MORE THAN
A PROPHET

THE IDENTITY OF JESUS FROM THE
BIBLE, QUR'AN AND EARLY SOURCES

JOHN STEWART

Mike —
Blessings!
[signature]
Rom. 8.28

More Than A Prophet
The Identity of Jesus From the Bible, Qur'an and Early Sources

© 2017 By John Stewart

ISBN: 978-1543210811

Published by Intelligent Faith Press
P.O. Box 186, Panora, Iowa 50216
www.IntelligentFaith.com

CONTENTS

Acknowledgments 5

Introduction 9

PART ONE: ATTRIBUTES OF GOD ASCRIBED TO JESUS 11

Chapter One: God Alone is the Creator 13

Chapter Two: God Alone Forgives Sins 21

Chapter Three: God Alone is Worshiped 27

Chapter Four: God Alone is the First and the Last 33

Chapter Five: God Alone Receives and Answer Prayers 39

Chapter Six: God Alone Gives Life 45

Chapter Seven: God Alone is the Final Judge of the Nations 49

Chapter Eight: God Alone is the "Truth" 53

Chapter Nine: No One Shares Glory with God 55

PART TWO: WHO JESUS, HIS FOLLOWERS AND HIS
ENEMIES SAID HE WAS 59

Chapter Ten: What Jesus' Followers Said About Him 61

Chapter Eleven: What Jesus' Enemies Said About Him 67

Chapter Twelve: What Early Christians Said About Jesus 71

Chapter Thirteen: What Jesus Said About Himself 75

PART THREE: QUESTIONS MUSLIMS ASK 85

Chapter Fourteen: How Can Jesus Have Limitations if He is God? 87

Chapter Fifteen: If Jesus is God, How Can God Die? 91

Chapter Sixteen: Did Jesus Say "I am God, Worship Me?" 95

Chapter Seventeen: Does the Old Testament Show Jesus is God? 99

Chapter Eighteen: Three Persons Called God, But One God? 105

Chapter Nineteen: What the Qur'an Says About the Bible 109

Chapter Twenty: If Jesus Is More Than A Prophet 121

Appendix One: Summary of God's Attributes 125

Appendix Two: The Gospel of Barnabas 129

Endnotes 141

Bibliography 147

About the Author 151

ACKNOWLEDGMENTS

No book is ever the work of one person. One person may have had the idea and then hovered over a computer for countless hours in efforts to bring the idea to life, but it takes many people for the idea to become a reality. Such is the case with *More Than A Prophet*. The genesis of this book was a number of lectures I gave on Christianity and Islam in such places as Indonesia, Australia, various countries in Africa, and across the United States. From audience reaction and comments it seemed appropriate to turn my lectures into writing because of a great hunger for the material. It has been my privilege to have the available time and means to write a book on such an important topic, and I hope that the evidence presented will help both Christians and Muslims understand *why* Jesus is *More Than A Prophet*. But before diving into the content, let me acknowledge the people who played a role in making this book happen.

First is my wife, Laurie. I thank her for her suggestions, comments and feedback, but also her encouragement and patience. It is a tremendous sacrifice for a wife to have her husband cloistered in his study for hours at a time working on a book, not knowing if she dares to interrupt for such underappreciated things as dinner. I hope that she views the final product as worth the sacrifice, especially with the knowledge that I couldn't have done it without her.

Next are the people whose writing, teaching and YouTube videos provided ideas and material for the book. This includes both Christians and Muslims. The Christian side of the ledger includes Nabeel Qureshi, David Wood, James White, Jay Smith, Darrell Furgason and my former colleague, the late Walter Martin. On the Muslim side, Shabir Ally provided the impetus for me to dig deeper into the subject of the deity of Jesus when he challenged me to a debate. As of this writing we are still working on the time and place to have our debate on "Is Jesus God?" Also, Sheikh Hussaini Yusuf Mabera, who graciously agreed to debate me in Lagos, Nigeria, where we had a lively exchange on the question of Jesus' deity. Sheikh Mabera's writings have helped me to more fully understand some of the issues Islamic apologists have with Christianity, and prompted me to address those issues formally in this book.

I must acknowledge the encouragement and inspiration received from my colleagues at Ratio Christi, the Student-Faculty Apologetic Alliance for whom I serve as Executive Director of its International arm. I am also grateful for the love and prayers freely given from so many at my home church in Iowa, and my former church in California.

Finally, many thanks to those who have followed Laurie and me on our faith journey and have supported the work we do. We stepped out in faith in 2005, making our first international mission trip to Nairobi, Kenya. Shortly thereafter we formed Rolling Stone Ministries and began travelling the world speaking on the evidence for the truth of Christianity. Along the way my heart ached for young people who lost their faith while attending the university, and I prayed that a door would open for me to help counter the increasing secularism and skepticism that was turning people away from Christianity. When I discovered the vision of Ratio Christi, it became apparent that we shared the same concerns, and I have been blessed to partner with them in presenting an intelligent Christian faith to the world. In my journeys I have witnessed firsthand the misconceptions that many traditional Muslims have about what Christianity teaches and what the Bible says about the person of Jesus. It is my heart's desire that Christians will find this book useful for talking with Muslims about the Jesus of the Bible, and that Muslims who read the book will understand who Jesus is according to Scripture, and will put their trust in the biblical, historical Jesus.

INTRODUCTION

When comparing two great world religions, Christianity and Islam, it is important to understand that they share common ground. Christians and Muslims agree there is One God, who created the universe. Both religions desire to worship the One God, obey his commandments and do his will. Christians and Muslims agree that there is an afterlife. Both affirm that Jesus of Nazareth was a prophet. The big difference is that Islam teaches that Jesus was merely a prophet, while Christianity teaches that Jesus was more than a prophet. Christianity teaches that Jesus was God incarnate, who came to earth, died on a cross for the sins of the world, and on the third day rose from the dead. Christianity also affirms that before becoming man at Bethlehem Jesus was the eternal Son of God, and God the Son.

On the question of the identity of Jesus—was he a mere prophet or God incarnate--Christianity and Islam cannot both be right (although both could be wrong). At least one view is wrong. In order to find out the truth about Jesus, this book investigates the relevant passages and claims found in the Bible, the Qur'an, and in the writings of early Christians. It is a search for truth, consistency and reason.

As we consider the evidence for the identity of Jesus, the following issues will be addressed:

- Attributes belonging solely to God ascribed to Jesus

- Who Jesus, his followers, enemies and early Christians said he was

- If Jesus is God, what about verses that show his limitations?

- If Jesus is God, and he died on a cross, how can God die?

- Did Jesus ever say, "I am God, worship me"?

- Is there evidence that God revealed himself in three persons?

- If Jesus was more than a prophet, what should we do?

When studying the life and teachings of Jesus, there are two separate aspects that are essential to understand: (1) Who he is, and (2) what he did. These two aspects are often referred to as Jesus' person and work. Although the person and work of Jesus are both essential topics for understanding the life and teachings of Jesus, this book deals primarily with his person, i.e., who Jesus is according to the Bible, the Qur'an and early Christian sources. The work of Jesus, which includes his death on a cross and resurrection from the dead, is vitally important, but an in depth investigation of those issues is beyond the scope of this book.

It is the author's prayer that readers will read this book with an open mind, interpret passages consistently, and follow the evidence wherever it leads. Evidence from Scripture, along with logic and reason, provides a sound basis to answer the eternally important question of whether Jesus was more than a prophet. May God open our hearts and minds to the Truth. *Inshallah.*

PART ONE

ATTRIBUTES OF GOD
ASCRIBED TO JESUS

CHAPTER ONE
God Alone is the Creator

Genesis 1:1   In the beginning God created the heavens and the earth.

Surah 13:16   Allah is the creator of all things.

Surah 35:3   Is there a Creator other than Allah?

Surah 42:11   (He is) the Creator of the heavens and the earth.

The human heart and mind want to know why we are here and whether this life is all there is. 17th century Philosopher Gottfried Leibniz famously asked, "Why is there something rather than nothing?" The fact that the universe is here and we are here does not answer the question of why we are here. Similarly, in the Bible Job asks the question, "If someone dies, will they live again?" (Job 14:14). The answers to Leibniz' and Job's questions have to come from outside the universe, because the universe does not provide the answers. Now that even skeptical scientists are affirming that universe had a beginning, there is more and more interest in learning about the creative force that began the universe. Humanity wants to know who is the Creator.

Christianity and Islam agree that God is the Creator of the universe. Neither the Bible nor the Qur'an explain how God created the universe out of nothing, nor when He created the universe. But the conclusion that God alone created the heavens and the earth is undisputed by Christianity and Islam. In Islam, "Creator" is one of 99 attributes (or, "titles") ascribed to God. As with Christianity, the attribute and title of being the Creator in Islam is a prerogative of deity, something not shared with the creation.

There are several Scriptural passages that are relevant in determining the answer to whether Jesus is the Creator or is a creation. First is John 1:1-3:

> In the beginning was the Word, and the Word was with God, and the Word was God. He was with God in the beginning. Through him all things were made; without him nothing was made that has been made.

John 1:1 introduces a Person called the "Word" (Greek *Logos*) who is said to be "face to face with God." The Greek preposition pros, translated "with," had a particular meaning in the Jewish culture in which the writer, John the Apostle, was raised. It portrays a "face to face" intimacy that occurred during a meal, or between husband and wife in the marriage bed. Thus, *pros* ("with") in John 1:1 meant much more than "alongside." The Word in John 1:1 enjoyed an intimacy with God, but, in addition, "the Word was God."

The Apostle John goes on to say that the Word "was with God in the beginning" (John 1:2), and is, therefore, eternal. Finally, John tells us that the Word is the creator, writing, "Through him all things were made; without him nothing was made that has been made" (John 1:3). The identity of this person called the Word, who is "face to face" with God, "is God," is eternal and is the Creator, is revealed in John 1:14: "The Word became flesh and made his dwelling among us. We have seen his glory, the glory of the one and only Son, who came from the Father, full of grace and truth." Clearly, Jesus is the Word, the one whom John says is God, is eternal and is the Creator.

John the Apostle identifies Jesus as God the Creator in John 1:3, then confirms this identification in John 1:10, "He was in the world, and though the world was made through him, the world did not recognize him." It would be hard to state the identity of the Creator any clearer than to say "The world was made through him" and "without him nothing was made that has been made" (John 1:3).

John 1:1-3 and John 1:10 are not the only passages in the Scripture that identify Jesus as the Creator. Paul echoes what the Apostle John wrote, writing in Colossians 1:16, "For in him all things were created: things in heaven and on earth, visible and invisible, whether thrones or powers or rulers or authorities; all things have been created through him and *for* him." Not only does the Apostle Paul present Jesus as the Creator, he adds that all things were created for Him. This is hardly a description of a mere prophet. How, indeed, could a mere prophet be the Creator and the beneficiary of creation?

Additionally, in Hebrews 1:2 we read that God "in these last days he has spoken to us by his Son, whom he appointed heir of all things, and through whom also he made the universe." Consistent with John 1:3, 10 and Colossians 1:16, here, again, Jesus is said to be the Creator of the universe.

In light of the foregoing passages, there is a question for those who were taught that Jesus is a mere prophet. Keep in mind the clear teachings of the Bible and Qur'an that God, alone, is the Creator of the universe, and that the title "Creator" is an attribute that belongs solely to God. With this in mind, if Jesus is a mere prophet:

How Can a Mere Prophet Be the Creator of the Universe?

Despite the Bible ascribing attributes of deity to Jesus, there are some who continue to deny the teachings of Jesus and the Bible. These people often feel a duty to explain away these teachings in order to maintain their beliefs. A case in point is a man I met on a pier in Santa Barbara, California who identified himself as a Jehovah's Witness. The man rejected the clear teaching that Jesus is the Creator (e.g., John 1:3, Colossians 1:16 and Hebrews 1:2), citing Colossians 1:15 in support, "The Son is the image of the invisible God, the firstborn over all creation." Some translations, such as the New World Translation of the Jehovah's Witnesses, read, "the firstborn *of* all creation." His point was that according to Colossians 1:15 Jesus is a creation, because he is called, "firstborn *of* all creation."

Just a few weeks before my conversation with the Jehovah's Witness on the pier, I engaged in a public debate/dialogue with a Muslim Sheikh on the question, "Is Jesus God?" The Sheikh, like the man in Santa Barbara, raised Colossians 1:15 to support the view that Jesus was created. I explained to both of these men that their view was erroneous, and I illustrated why they were wrong from a simple study of the Greek word Paul uses in Colossians 1:15 that is translated, "firstborn."

What I pointed out to the Sheikh and to the Jehovah's Witness was that the term the Apostle Paul uses in Colossians 1:15, "firstborn," is a translation of the Greek word *prototokos*. This term does not mean "first created." There is a simple Greek word, *protoktisis*, that means "first created." That is not the word Paul used in Colossians 1:15. Instead, he uses *prototokos*. What does this word mean?

Prototokos is a reference to priority (i.e., "firstness") in the sense of rank or position, not time. According to Kittel's Theological Dictionary of the New Testament, *prototokos* refers to "the unique supremacy of

Christ over all creatures as the Mediator of their creation."[1] This understanding of "firstborn" is supported by other Scriptures. For example, from Genesis 41:51-52 we learn that Joseph's "firstborn" (in sequence) was Manasseh, and Ephraim was second-born. However, in Jeremiah 31:9 it says, "Ephraim is my firstborn son." When Jeremiah 31:9 was translated from Hebrew into Greek (i.e., the "Septuagint"), the translators used the word *prototokos* when referring to Ephraim as "firstborn." From Genesis 41 and Jeremiah 31 it is clear that *prototokos*, as applied to Jesus in Colossians 1:15, refers figuratively to him as the firstborn of a new humanity. This usage of "firstborn" is also found in Romans 8:29, where Paul writes, "For those God foreknew he also predestined to be conformed to the image of his Son, that he might be the firstborn among many brothers and sisters." The word "firstborn" in Romans 8:29 is also a translation of the Greek word *prototokos*.

Finally, Psalm 89:27 says concerning David, "And I will appoint him to be my firstborn, the most exalted of the kings of the earth." The Septuagint (Greek) translation of Psalm 89:27 uses the Greek word *prototokos* for the word translated "firstborn." David was hardly God's firstborn in terms of sequence or order, but found great favor with the Lord, and is uniquely called "a man after his own heart" (1 Samuel 13:14). From the verses calling David and Ephraim "firstborn" it is estasblished that "firstborn" (*prototokos*) is used as a title for pre-eminence. Jesus, therefore, as *prototokos*, is pre-eminent over all creation according to Colossians 1:15, and is the Creator according to many verses, as set forth above.

Those who feel compelled, for one reason or another, to hold that Jesus was a created being commonly misconstrue Colossians 1:15. For example, Islamic scholar Shabir Ally writes,

Paul, believed to be the author of some thirteen or fourteen letters in the Bible, also believed that Jesus is not God. For

Paul, God first created Jesus, then used Jesus as the agent by which to create the rest of creation (see Colossians ch. 1, v. 15…).[2]

As previously discussed, Paul never said "God created Jesus." Instead, we find John the Apostle writing, "without him nothing was made that has been made" (John 1:3). If Jesus had been created John could not have said, "without him nothing was made that has been made."

Summary

In summarizing the question of the identity of the Creator, the teachings of both the Bible and the Qur'an are that God, alone, is the Creator. The term "Creator" is a title restricted to God, and is an attribute that belongs exclusively to God. That being the case, since the Bible also says through Jesus "all things were made," "the world was made by Him," "all things were created through Him," and "through [Jesus] [God] made the universe," it is also well supported that Jesus is the Creator. If God alone is the Creator, and Jesus is said to be the Creator,

How Can a Mere Prophet be the Creator?

Based on the biblical evidence that Jesus is the Creator, those who have been taught that Jesus is a mere prophet must either deny the teachings of multiple passages of Scripture in order to maintain that view, or else recognize that Jesus is more than a prophet. It has been said that sometimes the shallowness of the critic's argument speaks louder than the voice of the believer. A case in point is Ally's attempt to deny that Jesus is the Creator. On its face his view is fraught with problems, for how could a mere prophet be used by God "as the agent by which to create the rest of creation?" Recognizing Jesus as the agent of creation elevates him above the status of mortal man, but the Bible presents Jesus as much more than even an agent of creation. It presents Jesus as God, the Creator, for whom and through whom all things were created.

If God is the Creator, and Jesus is presented as the Creator, then Jesus must be God.

CHAPTER TWO
God Alone Forgives Sins

Isaiah 43:25:   [The LORD says] I, even I, am he who blots out your transgressions, for my own sake, and remembers your sins no more.

Daniel 9:9:   The Lord our God is merciful and forgiving, even though we have rebelled against him.

Micah 7:18:   Who is a God like you, who pardons sin....?

Surah 3:135:   ...and who can forgive sins except Allah?

Surah 39:53   Despair not of the mercy of Allah: for Allah forgives all sins....

As can be seen from the above-referenced passages, it is well established in both the Qur'an and the Bible that only God can forgive sins. Thus, the power to forgive sins is considered a prerogative of God alone. The dictionary defines "prerogative" as "an exclusive right or privilege."[1] This definition certainly applies to the question of who can forgive sins. Both the Bible and Qur'an have the same answer, namely that God, and God alone, forgives sins.

Anyone can claim to have the power to forgive sins, but unless the claimant is God, the claim constitutes "blasphemy," meaning "speaking injuriously about God" by allowing someone who is not

God to usurp his unique privileges. If someone does claim to have the power to forgive sins, the logical questions to ask are: "Who is this person claiming to have the power to forgive sins?" and "What evidence does the claimant provide as proof of the power to forgive sins?"

When Jesus was teaching at a house in Capernaum on the shore of the Sea of Galilee, the word was out that Jesus had great healing abilities. While he was teaching, a paralyzed man was carried to the house on a stretcher by four men, but the crowd inside the house was so large that the men could not get in. The men were persistent, and took the paralyzed man onto the roof, dug through the roofing material, and made an opening. They lowered the paralyzed man down with his stretcher into the center of the room where Jesus was teacher, ending up in front of Jesus.[2]

Jesus saw the faith of the men who brought their paralyzed friend, and said to the paralyzed man, "Friend, your sins are forgiven" (Luke 5:20). The scribes and Pharisees were aghast, thinking, "Who is this fellow who speaks blasphemy? Who can forgive sins but God alone?" (5:21). The scribes and Pharisees knew from the Old Testament Scriptures that conferring forgiveness of sins was a right that belonged only to God.

Jesus was aware of what they were thinking, and asked whether it was easier to say to the man "Your sins are forgiven" or "Get up and walk?" The obvious answer is that it's easier to say "Your sins are forgiven" because there is no way to verify whether a person's sins are actually forgiven since forgiveness happens in the unseen "spiritual realm." In short, if someone claims to confer forgiveness of sins, there is no way to empirically (i.e., with our senses) confirm whether forgiveness actually takes place. Thus, anyone can claim to forgive sins. What would not be easy to say to a paralyzed man is "Get up and walk." In a crowded room, such an order assumes the paralyzed man was healed.

That assumption could be tested. If the man did not get up, not only would Jesus' ability to heal be called into question, but his claim to forgive sins, if not his entire ministry, would rightly be rejected.

Jesus knew that merely asserting that the paralyzed man's sins were forgiven was not enough to convince the scribes and Pharisees. They had already asserted their position that only God can forgive sins, and since they did not believe that Jesus was God, his act of forgiving the paralytic was considered an act of blasphemy, namely the usurping of a right that belonged only to God. To convince the scribes and Pharisees of his power to forgive sins, Jesus had to provide them with tangible evidence, meaning something they could observe and verify. Thus, Jesus says, "I want you to know that the Son of Man has authority on earth to forgive sins." So he said to the paralyzed man, "I tell you, get up, take your mat and go home."[3]

Jesus linked his spiritual authority to forgive sins with the healing of the paralyzed man. Now all eyes are on the paralyzed man. Jesus' identity as the Messiah ("Christ") was on the line.[4] Either the man stays on his stretcher, which means Jesus is a pretender, a false teacher and blasphemer, or the man gets up, constituting empirical evidence that Jesus can forgive sins. Luke's account says regarding the paralyzed man, "Immediately he stood up in front of them, took what he had been lying on and went home praising God."[5] Jesus performed a miracle that was observed and verified by all those in the room. In light of the miracle, those watching had every reason to be convinced that Jesus had the authority to forgive sins.

The question for those who have been told that Jesus was a mere prophet is:

How could a mere prophet forgive sins, if only God is able to forgive sins?

Attempts to explain away Jesus' authority to forgive sins

Some people have been taught that Jesus is a mere prophet, or even that he is an angel.[6] When the passage about Jesus forgiving sins is presented, after having established that only God can forgive sins, the logical conclusion is that Jesus is more than a prophet. He is, in fact, God.

For those who want to maintain the view that Jesus is not God, it is incumbent on them to try to explain how Jesus forgave sins, since forgiveness is an acknowledged prerogative of deity found in both the Qur'an and the Bible. How, then, do those who see Jesus as a mere prophet try to explain away Jesus' authority to forgive sins? One example is Muslim scholar Shabir Ally's attempt to deny that Jesus had the power to forgive sins. He writes the following concerning the account of the paralytic to whom Jesus said, "Friend, your sins are forgiven:"

> What Jesus did here was as follows. Jesus announced to the man the knowledge Jesus received from God that God had forgiven the man. Notice Jesus did not say, 'I forgive your sins,' but rather, 'Your sins are forgiven,' implying, as this would to his Jewish listeners, that God had forgiven the man. Jesus, then, did not have the power to forgive sins....[7]

First, how would Jesus' statement "Your sins are forgiven" imply "to his Jewish listener, that God had forgiven the man?" Luke tells us that after Jesus forgave the man's sins, "The Pharisees and the teachers of the law began thinking to themselves, 'Who is this fellow who speaks blasphemy? Who can forgive sins but God alone?'" (Luke 5:21). What was actually implied by Jesus was that he possessed the power to forgive sins, and what was inferred by his Jewish listeners was that he was speaking blasphemy!

What Ally leaves out in his effort to spin the passage is that in all three Gospel accounts (Matthew, Mark and Luke) Jesus says, "So that you may know the *Son of Man* has power[8] on earth to forgive sins…." Jesus does not say, "So that you may know that *God* has power to forgive sins." Everyone listening to Jesus believed that God had the power to forgive sins. What they did not know was that Jesus had power to forgive sins. The reasonable conclusion is that either Jesus usurped the divine prerogative to forgive sins, or else He exercised the divine prerogative to forgive sins because he is God.

Those who have been taught that Jesus is a mere prophet have to answer the question of how a mere prophet can forgive sins if only God can forgive sins. It is unreasonable to cling to the tortured explanation that "Jesus did not have the power to forgive sins" when Jesus, Himself, said just the opposite: "So that you may know that the Son of Man has power on earth to forgive sins…." Thus, a plea for consistency is in order. Which explanation interprets the passage about Jesus healing the paralytic consistently—Jesus did not have the power to forgive sins or Jesus had the power to forgive sins? By taking Jesus at his word, the logical conclusion is he had the power to forgive sins. And if Jesus had that power, a power that belongs only to God according to the Bible, the Qur'an and even the religious leaders present at the house in Capernaum, then Jesus is more than a mere prophet.

If only God can forgive sins, and Jesus forgave sins, then Jesus must be God.

CHAPTER THREE
God Alone is Worshiped

Exodus 20:3, 5   You shall have no other gods before me…You
                  shall not bow down to them or worship them.

Luke 4:8   Jesus answered, "It is written: 'Worship the
                  Lord your God and serve him only.'"

Surah 3:64   Say: "O people of the Book! Come to common
                  terms as between us and you: that we worship
                  none but Allah…."

Surah 17:22, 23   Take not with Allah another object of
                  worship…Thy Lord hath decreed that ye
                  worship none but Him…."

The dictionary defines worship as "reverent love and devotion to a deity."[1] The Bible and the Qur'an are in agreement that God, and God alone, is to be worshiped. No mere prophet or human being is entitled to worship. This principle is illustrated from several New Testament accounts.

First, a devout centurion named Cornelius had a vision in which the Lord told him to send for the Apostle Peter. Cornelius dispatched men from his town of Caesarea to find Peter in Joppa. They found Peter and brought him to Cornelius. According to Acts 10:25-26,[2] when

Peter arrived, "Cornelius met him, and fell at his feed and worshiped him. But Peter raised him up, saying, "Stand up; I too am just a man.""

Next, in Acts chapter 14 the Apostle Paul healed a man in the town of Lystra who had been lame from birth. The crowd saw the healing, and began saying, ""The gods have come down to us in human form!" (Acts 14:11). The crowd then gave Paul and Barnabas the names of Roman gods, and wanted to offer sacrifices to them. When Paul and Barnabas heard what was happening "they tore their clothes and rushed out into the crowd, shouting: 'Friends, why are you doing this? We too are only human, like you. We are bringing you good news, telling you to turn from these worthless things to the living God, who made the heavens and the earth and the sea and everything in them.'"

Finally, in the Book of Revelation chapter 22, an angel shows the Apostle John a vision of heaven. John says, "I, John, am the one who heard and saw these things. And when I had heard and seen them, I fell down to worship at the feet of the angel who had been showing them to me." But the angel said to John, "Don't do that! I am a fellow servant with you and with your fellow prophets and with all who keep the words of this scroll. Worship God!"

In all three accounts the response was to reject the worship offered to them because none of the recipients was God. These are the responses that both Christianity and Islam demand if worship is offered to someone other than God. With this in mind, there are several accounts in the Gospels where Jesus is worshiped. How did Jesus respond when others worshiped him?

Jesus' response to receiving worship

In Matthew chapter 14, Jesus walked on water, and when he got into the boat with the disciples, Matthew writes, "Then those who were in the boat worshiped him, saying, 'Truly you are the Son of God'" (14:33).

Based on how Peter responded to Cornelius' worship, how Paul and Barnabas responded to the worship by the people in Lystra, and how the angel responded to John's worship, if Jesus was just a mere man or fellow servant, he should have said to the disciples, "Don't worship me," but he does not. He received worship from them without any correction, clarification or rebuke.

Similarly, in Matthew 28:9, as the women were returning from Jesus' empty tomb Jesus met them and greeted them, and "They came to him, clasped his feet and worshiped Him." Jesus says nothing to indicate their worship of him was wrong or improper.

In Matthew 28:17, after Jesus rose from the dead He met His disciples in Galilee, and "When they saw Him they worshiped him…." Again Jesus does not tell the disciples, "Don't worship me." Instead, he tells them, "All authority in heaven and on earth has been given to me" (28:17), then adds, "Therefore go and make disciples of all nations, baptizing them in the name of the Father and of the Son and of the Holy Spirit" (28:19). Rather than deflect the worship being offered to him, Jesus tells the disciples that he has "all authority in heaven and on earth," and that new disciples are to be baptized "in the name of the Father and of the Son and of the Holy Spirit," putting himself on equal footing with God the Father.

Finally, in John chapter nine Jesus healed a man blind from birth. Jesus asked the man whether he believes in the Son of Man, to which the formerly blind man says, "Who is he, sir? Tell me so that I may believe in him (9:36). Jesus said, 'You have now seen him; in fact, he is the one speaking with you.' (9:37). Then the man said, 'Lord, I believe,' and he worshiped him." (9:38). In the accounts of the disciples in the boat, the women returning from the empty tomb and the disciples after Jesus' resurrection, Jesus receives worship without comment. No mention of a mistake, no limitation mentioned, not even a slight pause.

Why would Peter, Paul and Barnabas, and the angel go out of their way to correct their worshipers while over and over again Jesus remained silent when he was worshiped? Jesus knew better than anyone what the Scriptures said about worship, and when the devil wanted to receive worship from Jesus, Jesus quotes Deuteronomy 6:13, "It is written: 'Worship the Lord your God and serve him only'" (Luke 4:8).

In light of Jesus' silent acceptance of worship, there are two possibilities: First, Jesus was a mere prophet, not entitled to worship, but lacked the character shown by Peter, Paul and Barnabas and the angel when he failed to tell his worshipers to stop. That would make Jesus guilty of usurping the adoration that belongs solely to God, a classic example of "blasphemy." The second possibility is that Jesus was entitled to worship because he was more than prophet. Given the character of Jesus as shown throughout the Gospels, the first possibility, namely that Jesus knew he was not entitled to worship but silently accepted it anyway, falls under its own weight. The second possibility, that Jesus was entitled to worship, is the only coherent conclusion. And if Jesus, his disciples, the women and the man born blind all believed he was entitled to worship, then it follows that they all believed he was God.

Additional accounts of Jesus being worshiped

In Matthew 2:2 the Magi from the East ask, "Where is the one who has been born king of the Jews? We saw his star when it rose and have come to worship him." Matthew 2:11 says the Magi "bowed down and worshiped him." Matthew's account says nothing about the Magi's worship being improper. Further, in Luke 24 Jesus has parting words for the disciples, then he ascends into heaven. Following his ascension Luke writes, "Then they worshiped him and returned to Jerusalem with great joy" (Luke 24:52). Luke gives no indication that the disciples' worship was improper or misguided. If Jesus was not entitled to worship, why didn't Matthew or Luke set the record straight? The reasonable conclusion is that their silence is an endorsement that Jesus is to be worshiped because he is more than a prophet—he is God incarnate.

The Father commands worship of Jesus

One of the clearest passages supporting the position that Jesus was entitled to worship is found in the prologue to the letter to the Hebrews. The letter begins by God the Father asserting that he has spoken to humanity by his Son:

> In the past God spoke to our ancestors through the prophets at many times and in various ways, but in these last days he has spoken to us by his Son, whom he appointed heir of all things, and through whom also he made the universe. The Son is the radiance of God's glory and the exact representation of his being, sustaining all things by his powerful word. After he had provided purification for sins, he sat down at the right hand of the Majesty in heaven. So he became as much superior to the angels as the name he has inherited is superior to theirs. For to which of the angels did God ever say, "You are my Son; today I have become your Father"? Or again, "I will be his Father, and he will be my Son"? (Hebrews 1:1-5).

From this passage we learn several things: First, God has spoken in the last days "by his Son" (Hebrews 1:2). Next, his Son "has been appointed heir of all things," and is the agent through whom the universe was made (1:2). Further, the Son "is the radiance of God's glory" (1:3), and is the "exact representation" of God's being (1:3). Finally, the Son is also "superior to the angels" (1:4) because God has called Him "My Son" (1:5).

Hebrews 1:1-5 make a case for the uniqueness of Jesus as the Creator, the heir of everything, who represents God's being and radiates God's glory, and who is much superior to the angels because he is God's Son. These verses elevate Jesus to a status far above that of a mere prophet, but the next verse explains just how much more than a prophet Jesus is: "And again, when God brings his firstborn into the world, he says, "Let all God's angels worship him" (Hebrews 1:6).

Worship? God the Father commands that Jesus is to receive worship? Since both the Bible and Qur'an make clear that only God is to be worshiped, here is the question for those who have been told that Jesus is a mere prophet:

Why would God the Father command that a mere prophet be worshiped?

The Greek word in Hebrews 1:6 translated "worship" is *proskuneo*. This verb refers to reverence or worship paid "to God…of the God worshiped by monotheists…."[3] *Proskuneo* is the same word used in Luke 4:8, where Jesus says, "Worship the Lord your God and serve him only."[4] As if God telling the angels to worship Jesus is not enough, Hebrews 1:8 continues with what God says: "But about the Son he says, 'Your throne, O God, will last for ever and ever; a scepter of justice will be the scepter of your kingdom.'" God the Father refers to Jesus as "God," and says Jesus has an eternal throne. Perhaps this is the clearest explanation as to why Jesus is worshipped—He is more than a mere prophet.

The foregoing accounts make clear that God the Father told angels to worship Jesus and that Jesus received worship while he was on earth. Since only God is to be worshipped, and since Jesus is worshipped, it is clear that Jesus is presented in the Bible as more than a mere prophet. Simply put,

If only God is to be worshiped, and Jesus was worshiped, then Jesus is God.

CHAPTER FOUR
God Alone is the First and the Last

Isaiah 44:6   This is what the LORD says—Israel's King and Redeemer, the LORD Almighty: I am the first and I am the last; apart from me there is no God.

Surah 57:1, 3   Whatever is in the heavens and on earth—let it declare the Praise and Glory of Allah…He is the First and the Last….

Both Islamic and Christian scholars refer to God as eternal. "Eternal" is understood as meaning uncreated, pre-existent and without end. The verses cited above ascribe the title of "First and Last" to God as indicative of his eternal nature. The title "First and Last" does not mean God is the first in a sequence and the last in a sequence, nor does it mean that he had a beginning or will have an end. Despite the difficulty of the human mind to grasp the concept of a divine being that has always existed, the fact that Islam and Christianity teach the eternal nature of God is undisputed.

The question of whether Jesus is a more than a prophet can be answered, at least in part, by asking whether the Bible teaches that Jesus is eternal. In short, did Jesus pre-exist from eternity past, or was he created at some point?

There are many passages that help answer the question of Jesus' pre-existence. Before dealing with those texts, let us revisit what is established from both the Qur'an and the Bible, namely, that God is the First and the Last. In a rational universe, there can only be one First and one Last. As my former colleague, the late Walter Martin, used to say, "To have two 'Firsts' and two 'Lasts' is linguistic suicide."

In the New Testament, in the Book of Revelation, chapter one, a person appears to the Apostle John that he describes as "like a son of man" (1:13). The person places His right hand on John and says, "Do not be afraid. I am the First and the Last" (1:17). The person goes on to say, "I am the Living One; I was dead, and now look, I am alive for ever and ever...." (1:18). The identification of this person John envisions can be determined by John's use of "son of man," a title Jesus uses for himself in many passages in the Gospels,[1] and the reference to "I was dead, and now look, I am alive for ever and ever." "Son of man" together with being dead and now being alive, uniquely applies to Jesus.

As further evidence of this person's identity, in Revelation 22:13-14 there is another reference to someone saying he is the "First and Last:" "Look, I am coming soon! My reward is with me, and I will give to each person according to what they have done. I am the Alpha and the Omega, the First and the Last, the Beginning and the End." In Revelation 22:16 the speaker in verses 13-14 is identified, saying, "I Jesus." Therefore, twice in the Book of Revelation Jesus is called the "First and the Last." Should a mere prophet be using a title for himself that is applied only to God? Since God alone is the First and the Last, here is a question for those who were taught that Jesus is a mere prophet:

Why is Jesus called the "First and the Last?"

A related question to the identity of the "First and the Last" is the question of Jesus' pre-existence. Historic Christianity affirms that Jesus pre-existed as the Son (or, the "Word") before becoming flesh at Bethlehem.[2] There are several passages that relate, directly or indirectly, to this question.

Passages that Address Jesus' Pre-existence

John 1:1 says, "In the beginning was the Word, and the Word was with God, and the Word was God." John 1:14 says, "The Word became flesh and made his dwelling among us." Taken together, John 1:1 and 1:14 clearly teach that the Word (Greek *Logos*) was "in the beginning" and then became flesh, an explicit teaching that the Word pre-existed before taking on a human form. The taking on flesh, called the "incarnation," refers to the act of God becoming man at Bethlehem for the purpose of giving his life as a ransom for many (see Matthew 20:28).

In John 1:15, John the Baptist says regarding Jesus, "He who comes after me has surpassed me because he was before me." Since John was born before Jesus (see Luke chapters 1 and 2), this can only mean that Jesus pre-existed John. John 3:13 says Jesus, the "son of man," "came from heaven." Jesus repeatedly uses the expression "I have come" in the Gospels (e.g., Matthew 5:17, Matthew 10:34-35, Mark 2:17, Mark 10:45, Luke 12:49, Luke 19:10). The natural sense of these passages is that Jesus came from heaven, as stated in John 3:13. These verses, therefore, are evidence of his pre-existence as the Son. Additionally, in John 6:38 Jesus says, "For I have come down from heaven not to do my will but to do the will of him who sent me." It is difficult to imagine any interpretation of these verses that does not affirm Jesus' pre-existence.

The concept that Christ pre-existed in heaven before becoming man at Bethlehem is confirmed in John 6:62 where Jesus asks, "Then what if you see the Son of Man ascend to where he was before!" Further, in John 8:14 Jesus says, "I know where I came from and where I am going" and in John 8:23 Jesus said, "You are from below; I am from above. You are of this world; I am not of this world.". In John 8:58 Jesus says, "Very truly I tell you," Jesus answered, "before Abraham was born, I am!" This verse only makes sense if Jesus existed before Abraham.

In John 17:5, Jesus prays to the Father, saying, "And now, Father, glorify me in your presence with the glory I had with you before the world began." Not only does this indicate Jesus pre-existed, but it also shows that Jesus shared glory with the Father in eternity past. Similarly, in John 17:24 Jesus said, "Father, I want those you have given me to be with me where I am, and to see my glory, the glory you have given me because you loved me before the creation of the world."

In Paul's writings there are several verses that support Jesus' pre-existence. In 1 Corinthians 10:4 Paul discusses the children of Israel wandering in the wilderness, and writes, "they drank from the spiritual rock that accompanied them, and that rock was Christ." Further, in 1 Corinthians 15:47 Paul contrasts Adam and Jesus, writing, "The first man was of the dust of the earth; the second man is of heaven." Paul, then, confirms what the Gospels repeatedly teach, namely that Jesus is from heaven, and pre-existed before becoming man.

Paul also appears to confirm what Jesus said in John 17:5 regarding Him having glory with the Father before the foundation of the world. In 2 Corinthians 8:9 Paul writes concerning Jesus, "For you know the grace of our Lord Jesus Christ, that though he was rich, yet for your sake he became poor, so that you through his poverty might become rich." When was Jesus rich? Not during his early ministry. This can only be a reference to Jesus leaving the glory of heaven to come to earth, a teaching that Paul explains in greater detail in Philippians 2:5-11 (see below).

In Galatians 4:4, Paul writes, "But when the set time had fully come, God sent his Son, born of a woman, born under the law." This verse implies that the Son pre-existed, and was sent to earth at the appropriate time.

In Philippians 2:5-11 Paul passes along what most Bible scholars see as a primitive hymn to Christ. He writes,

> …have the same mindset as Christ Jesus: Who, being in the very nature God, did not consider equality with God something to be used to his own advantage; rather, he made himself nothing by taking the very nature of a servant, being made in human likeness. And being found in appearance as a man, he humbled himself by becoming obedient to death—even death on a cross!

From this we find that before becoming flesh Christ had the "nature of God," shared "equality with God," and took "the very nature of a servant, being made in human likeness." The logical conclusion is that Christ had the nature of God before the incarnation, solid evidence for his pre-existence and divinity. In Colossians 1:17 Paul writes, "He is before all things, and in him all things hold together." Being "before all things" also is reasonably understood as teaching that Jesus pre-existed, and is eternal.

The writer to the Hebrews provides another verse that supports Christ's pre-existence. Hebrews 10:5 reads, "Wherefore when he cometh into the world, he saith, 'a body hast thou prepared me.'" This is most naturally understood as another reference to the incarnation as set forth in John 1:1 and 1:14.

Jude verse 25 says, "to the only God our Savior be glory, majesty, power and authority, through Jesus Christ our Lord, before all ages, now and forevermore! Amen." "Before all ages" implies the pre-existence of Christ.

Finally, there is an Old Testament reference that is considered by many to be a prophecy of the Messiah. Micah 5:2 says, "But you, Bethlehem Ephrathah, though you are small among the clans of Judah, out of you will come for me one who will be ruler over Israel, whose origins are from of old, from ancient times." If this is, indeed, a reference to the coming Christ, then Christ's origins are "from old, from ancient times," an inference to the pre-existence of the Messiah.

No Christian or Muslim disputes that God is the First and the Last, and that he is eternal, not created. Jesus is called the "First and the Last," and in numerous places he is said to have existed before the foundation of the world. These texts are not isolated to one writer. The pre-existence and eternal existence of Jesus, the Son, can be found in all four Gospels, 1 and 2 Corinthians, Galatians, Philippians, Colossians, Hebrews, Jude and Revelation. The logical conclusion, from Jesus' own words and those of his followers, is that he is more than a mere prophet. The Scriptural evidence reveals Jesus as God, the First and the Last, who pre-existed as the Son, and is referred to as God the "Word" ("*Logos*"), who became flesh and made his dwelling among us.

If God alone is the First and the Last, and if Jesus is the First and the Last, then Jesus is God.

The most reasonable conclusion to passages that call Jesus "First and Last" and either assert or imply his pre-existence is that Jesus is more than a prophet. According to the teachings of the Bible, Jesus is God, the eternal Son, who became a man at Bethlehem so that he might bear the sins of humanity, thereby offering forgiveness to all who put their trust in him. These truths are summarized in John 3:16: "For God so loved the world that he gave his one and only Son, that whoever believes in him shall not perish but have eternal life."

CHAPTER FIVE
God Alone Receives and Answers Prayer

Genesis 25:21   Isaac prayed to the LORD on behalf of his wife, because she was childless. The LORD answered his prayer.

Psalm 50:15   Call on Me in the day of trouble; I will deliver you, and you will honor me.

Surah 2:186   I listen to the prayer of every suppliant when he calleth on Me.

Surah 40:60   And your Lord says: "Call on Me; I will answer your (prayer).

Prayers are part of the practice of virtually all religions. In Islam, according to the Hadith,[1] prayers are to be offered five times per day to God. In Christianity, followers of Jesus are told to "pray continually" (1 Thessalonians 5:17). Prayers, as taught in the Qur'an and the Bible, are directed toward God, and God alone. Directing prayers to anyone else constitutes blasphemy and idolatry. So, what does the Bible say concerning Jesus and prayers?

Prayers to the Father

Matthew chapters 5-7 records Jesus' famous "Sermon on the Mount." In this teaching Jesus explains that prayer is not for "show," and provides the disciples with a model for prayers, saying, "This, then, is how you should pray: 'Our Father in heaven, hallowed be your name....'" According to Jesus, prayers to God are to be directed to God the Father. Jesus followed this practice, as can be seen in his lengthy prayer to the Father recorded in John chapter 17, which begins, "After Jesus said this, he looked toward heaven and prayed: 'Father, the hour has come. Glorify your Son, that your Son may glorify you.'" Praying to God the Father was Jesus' pattern throughout his recorded ministry. The Apostle Paul confirms this practice, adding a small detail: "And whatever you do, whether in word or deed, do it all in the name of the Lord Jesus, giving thanks to God the Father through him" (Colossians 3:17).

Paul's addition of "giving thanks to God the Father through [Jesus]" lends Scriptural support to the concept that we have access to God the Father because of Jesus' sacrifice on the cross. Paul repeats this idea in Ephesians 3:12, "In him and through faith in him we may approach God with freedom and confidence." Where did this notion come from that holds we can access God the Father because of what Jesus did on our behalf? It came from Jesus himself, who said in John 14:6, "No one comes to the Father except through me," and in John 16:23, "In that day you will no longer ask me anything. Very truly I tell you, my Father will give you whatever you ask in my name." Thus, praying "in Jesus' name" is a principle taught by Jesus himself.

Prayers to Jesus

In Acts chapters six and seven, Steven, a follower of Jesus, was performing great wonders and signs among the people. Some Jews tried to argue with Stephen, but they could not cope with his wisdom, so they secretly induced men to say that Stephen blasphemed Moses and God. As a result, he was literally dragged before the Jewish High Court ("Sanhedrin"), and the accusers put forward false witnesses who claimed Stephen had spoken against the temple and the Law. Stephen was asked if the charges were true, and he eloquently responded, denying the charges, and testifying as to why Jesus was the Messiah that the Jewish prophets had predicted. Stephen added that the Jews historically persecuted God's prophets, and that they did not keep the Law ordained by angels. Those remarks caused the Jews to attack Stephen, then drive him out of Jerusalem where they stoned him. Acts 7:59 says, "While they were stoning him, Stephen prayed, 'Lord Jesus, receive my spirit.'"

When Stephen offered a prayer to Jesus he not only implied a belief that Jesus hears prayers, but also implies a confidence that Jesus had the ability to "receive" his spirit. Following his first request, i.e., that Jesus would receive his spirit, Stephen "fell on his knees and cried out, 'Lord, do not hold this sin against them.'" Inherent in Stephen's final request was his further belief that Jesus had the power to not charge those participating in his martyrdom with sin. It should not escape our attention that this prayer was uttered in the presence of "a young man named Saul" (Acts 7:58), who became the Apostle Paul. From this account in Acts we see that Paul had an early experience with the followers of Jesus praying not just in Jesus' name, but also praying to Jesus.

Another example of prayers directed to Jesus is in 1 Corinthians 1:2. In the salutation to the Christians in Corinth, Paul writes, "To the church of God in Corinth, to those sanctified in Christ Jesus and called to be his holy people, together with all those everywhere who call on the name of our Lord Jesus Christ." The expression "call on the name of our Lord Jesus Christ" refers to the Corinthian believers praying to

Jesus. Popular 19th century Bible expositor Alexander MacLaren comments on 1 Corinthians 1:2:

> Prayer to Christ from the very beginning of the Christian Church was, then, the characteristic of believers, and He to whom they prayed, thus, from the beginning, was recognised by them as being a Divine Person, God manifest in the flesh.[2]

In John 14:13-14 Jesus told his disciples, "And I will do whatever you ask in my name, so that the Father may be glorified in the Son. You may ask me for anything in my name, and I will do it." "Asking" in Jesus' name is a reference to praying to God the Father in Jesus' name. But Jesus also says, "You may ask me for anything in my name and I will do it." Thus, Jesus permits prayers to be offered to himself and also answers those prayers.

In light of Stephen praying to Jesus, the Corinthians praying to Jesus, and Jesus himself approving of his followers praying to him, a question arises for those who have been taught that Jesus is a mere prophet:

Why would anyone pray to a mere prophet, and how could a mere prophet answer prayer?

There is no dispute between Islam and Christianity that prayers are to be offered to God alone, and that God alone answers prayer. Yet the Bible clearly teaches that prayers are offered to Jesus, and Jesus claims that he can answer prayer. The teachings of the Bible show Jesus either as a blasphemer and usurper of divine prerogatives, or else someone who has the right to receive and answer prayer. If Jesus does, as the Scriptures teach, have the right to receive and answer prayer, then the only proper conclusion is that he is more than a prophet. Jesus enjoys the divine prerogative of receiving and answering prayers. The inescapable conclusion for those who take seriously what Jesus said and what others said about him is seen in the following syllogism:

Since only God is to be prayed to and answers prayers, and since Jesus is prayed to and answers prayers, Jesus is God.

CHAPTER SIX
God Alone Gives Life

1 Samuel 2:5   The LORD brings death and makes alive; he brings down to the grave and raises up.

Psalm 36:9   You are the one who gives and sustains life. (NET version)

Surah 22:7   And verily the Hour will come: there can be no doubt about it, or about (the fact) that Allah will raise up all who are in the graves.

Surah 7:158   It is He that giveth both life and death.

"Life Giver" is one of Allah's 99 names according to Islam. Similarly, the Bible says that God is the one who gives and sustains life. From these teachings one can conclude that in both Christianity and Islam God alone is the giver of life. No one but God, therefore, can legitimately claim to be a giver of life.

Jesus as Life Giver

John 1:4 says concerning Jesus, "In him was life." This principle is further developed in John chapter four, where Jesus tells a Samaritan woman that he offers "living water" (4:10), and "whoever drinks the water I give them will never thirst. Indeed, the water I give them will become in them a spring of water welling up to eternal life" (4:14). In this passage it is Jesus giving the water that wells up to eternal life. The full scope of Jesus as a Life Giver is unveiled in John chapter five. In 5:21 Jesus says, "For just as the Father raises the dead and gives them life, even so the Son gives life to whom he is pleased to give it." Since Jesus says that he "gives life" to whom he is pleased to give it, the question for those who have been taught that Jesus is a mere prophet is:

Should a mere prophet claim that he gives life to whomever he pleases?

Another way of addressing the question of whether a mere prophet could claim to be the "giver of life," is to recall that "Life Giver" is a title restricted to God. Since Jesus says he is a "life giver," then if he is a mere prophet he is a blasphemer who has usurped a divine title. But if he is truly a life giver, and if only God is a life giver, then Jesus is claiming to possess an attribute of deity. The inescapable conclusion is that Jesus is claiming to be God.

Jesus claims he will raise himself from the dead

A life-giver includes someone who raises the dead. Thus, resurrections of the dead are within the exclusive province of God. In a debate I had with a Muslim apologist, the topic of the resurrection came up. The Muslim apologist adamantly asserted that, according to the Bible "God raised Jesus from the dead." In order to make a point about Jesus claiming to be God, I asked, "You agree that God raised Jesus from the dead?" He nodded, repeating, "Yes, God raised Jesus from the dead."

Once I had established that God raised Jesus from the dead, I then asked him to read any English translation of John 2:19 and 2:21. He read the verses: "Jesus answered them, 'Destroy this temple, and I will raise it again in three days' (2:19)... But the temple he had spoken of was his body" (2:21). Just to drive the point home, I asked him to read the verses again, which he did. I merely said, "So, according to Jesus, he raised himself from the dead." The inference was clear—if God raised Jesus from the dead, and Jesus raised himself from the dead, then Jesus must be God. Therefore, in light of what Jesus said about raising himself from the dead, the question for those who think Jesus was a mere prophet is:

How could a mere prophet raise himself from the dead?

The simplest answer to the question is, "A mere prophet couldn't raise himself from the dead." Thus, all the evidence points to Jesus being more than a mere prophet. The evidence points to him having prerogatives belonging to God alone.

We must come to Jesus for life

According to the Bible we are all sinners (Roman 3:23) and the wages of sin is death (Romans 6:23). The only remedy for death is life, and Jesus said, " I have come that they may have life" (John 10:10). But Jesus also said that many people who study the Scriptures think that they have life, but without coming to him they don't have life. Jesus admonished, "You study the Scriptures diligently because you think that in them you have eternal life. These are the very Scriptures that testify about me" (John 5:39), then added, "yet you refuse to come to me to have life" (John 5:40).

Jesus explained what is necessary to have life: "Very truly I tell you, whoever hears my word and believes him who sent me has eternal life and will not be judged but has crossed over from death to life" (John 5:24). Jesus went on to say that he is "the bread of life" (John 6:48) and "This bread is my flesh, which I will give for the life of the world" (John 6:51). Those who believe Jesus was a prophet of God should take him at his word and believe in him for eternal life.

Over and over again Jesus says the he is the one who gives eternal life to those who believe. In John 10:28 he says concerning his "sheep,"

"I give them eternal life, and they shall never perish; no one will snatch them out of my hand." Jesus as the Life Giver is further illustrated in an account found in John chapter 11. When Jesus was returning to Bethany on the outskirts of Jerusalem he was met by Martha, whose brother Lazarus had died four days earlier. Martha told Jesus that had he been there her brother would not have died. Jesus said to her, "I am the resurrection and the life. The one who believes in me will live, even though they die; and whoever lives by believing in me will never die" (John 11:25-26). Jesus then proceeded to raise Lazarus from the dead. These words and deeds illustrate what Jesus meant when he told his disciples, "I am the life" (John 14:6). These are not the words and deeds of a mere prophet.

Islam and Christianity both affirm that God is the Life Giver, yet the Bible clearly teaches that Jesus claimed to "give life" to whomever he pleases (John 5:21). Not only does Jesus have the power to give life to all who believe (John 5:24), he also claimed to have the power to raise himself from the dead (John 2:19, 21). In light of Jesus' own claims, the obvious conclusion is that he was more than a prophet. His words and actions demonstrate that as the "Life Giver" Jesus is God the Son.

CHAPTER SEVEN
God Alone Is the Final Judge of the Nations

Psalm 96:13   Let all creation rejoice before the LORD, for he comes, he comes to judge the earth. He will judge the world in righteousness and the peoples in his faithfulness.

Surah 22:56-57   On that Day the Dominion will be that of Allah: He will judge between them: so those who believe and work righteous deeds will be in Gardens of Delight. And for those who reject Faith and deny Our Signs, there will be a humiliating punishment.

Christianity and Islam both view God as the final judge. It is God, and God alone, that determines who will enter into a blissful afterlife, and who will be punished. Psalm 110:6 reads, "He will judge the nations."

As a lawyer, I have great respect for those who wear the robes of a judge, realizing the awesome responsibility they have when they make rulings that effect people's lives. I haven't always agree with the decisions of judges whom I appeared before, but I always endeavored to give judges due respect. Spending time in courts of law has taught me that in this life there is no such thing as "perfect justice." However, there is a Judge who knows all the facts, and nothing is hidden from him. In this life we should still do our best to pursue justice for all, but perfect justice comes from God, and God alone.

Jesus had many things to day regarding judging and justice. He rebuked those who were quick to condemn, especially those who found a speck in their brothers' eye when they had a log in their own (Matthew 7:1-5). Jesus said regarding judgments on the human level, "Stop judging by mere appearances, but instead judge correctly" (John 7:24). Jesus elevated God's judgment to include not just spoken words ("… everyone will have to give account on the day of judgment for every empty word they have spoken") (Matthew 12:36), but even thoughts of the heart ("anyone who looks at a woman lustfully has already committed adultery with her in his heart") (Matthew 5:28).

The Final Judge of the nations

When discussing divine judgment, Jesus said in John 5:22, "The Father judges no one, but has entrusted all judgment to the Son." Further, in Matthew 25:31-32, Jesus said, "When the Son of Man comes in his glory, and all the angels with him, he will sit on his glorious throne. All the nations will be gathered before him, and he will separate the people one from another as a shepherd separates the sheep from the goats." If God is going to judge the nations, why has the Father entrusted all judgment to the Son, and why is Jesus seen as judging the nations?

From John 5:22 and Matthew 25:31-32 it is clear that Jesus is going to be the judge of all the earth, yet in Genesis 18:25 God is called "the Judge of all the earth" and in 1 Samuel 2:10 it says, "the "LORD will judge the ends of the earth." If God is the Judge of all the earth, and Jesus is the judge of all the earth, then "God" includes Jesus. Jesus, therefore, is more than a prophet. He is the God who will judge the nations. For those who have been told that Jesus is a mere prophet, the question is:

How can a mere prophet be the final judge of the nations?

Judging our secrets

In Romans chapter two the Apostle Paul discusses how God has written His law into the hearts of all people, so that their conscience confirms when they do right and accuses them when they do wrong (2:15). Following this, Paul writes, "This will take place on the day when God judges people's secrets through Jesus Christ" (2:16). According to Paul, Jesus is the one who through whom God the Father will judge the thoughts and actions of people. This confirms what Jesus himself said, as noted above. No mere prophet can judge the thoughts and actions of all people. Such a task is only possible if the Judge is divine.

CHAPTER EIGHT
God Alone Is the "Truth"

John 3:33   God is truthful.

Psalm 31:5 KJV Into thine hand I commit my spirit: thou hast redeemed me, O LORD God of truth.

Surah 10:82   And Allah by His Words doth prove and establish His truth.

The Bible and the Qur'an agree that God determines truth. In fact, one of the names for God in Islam is "Truth." "Truth" is often defined as "that which conforms with fact or reality." In the Qur'an, Surah 22:6 says, "That is so, because Allah is the Reality." Hence, God is seen in both Christianity and Islam as being the embodiment of truth, and whatever he does or says conforms with fact or reality.

Jesus and the truth

The Apostle John wrote in his Gospel concerning Jesus, "We have seen his glory, the glory of the one and only Son, who came from the Father, full of grace and truth" (John 1:14). John also writes, "For the law was given through Moses; grace and truth came through Jesus Christ" (John 1:17). Jesus had much to say about "truth." He said, God is spirit, and his worshipers must worship in the Spirit and in truth" (John 4:24). In John 8:32 Jesus said, "Then you will know the truth, and the truth will set you free."

Jesus also claimed that he always told the truth (e.g., John 8:45-46). Finally, when Jesus was interrogated by Roman Prefect Pontius Pilate the night before his crucifixion, he told Pilate, "the reason I was born and came into the world is to testify to the truth. Everyone on the side of truth listens to me" (John 18:37). Since both Islam and Christianity accept that Jesus is a prophet, then his words ought to be heeded.

What else did Jesus say about truth? The most revealing statement he made is found in John 14:6: "Jesus answered, 'I am the way and the truth and the life. No one comes to the Father except through me.'" Jesus claimed to do more than tell the truth—Jesus said that he was the Truth.

If God is a God of truth, and if "Truth" is a title that belongs only to God, then if Jesus called Himself "the Truth," is he not claiming to be God? Asked another way:

How could a mere prophet call himself the "Truth?"

John 14:6 is another example of Jesus applying to himself a name or title that belongs to God. No mere prophet should usurp names that belong exclusively to God. This creates a dilemma. Jesus is either a usurper of divine names if he is a mere prophet or else he is entitled to use divine names for himself because he is more than a prophet. Since the cumulative evidence supports the conclusion that Jesus was more than a prophet, a seeker of truth ought to admit there is substantial evidence that Jesus is God.

CHAPTER NINE
No One Shares Glory with God

Isaiah 42:8   "I am the LORD; that is my name! I will not yield my glory to another."

Surah 57:1   Whatever is in the heavens and on earth—let it declare the Praise and Glory of Allah.

The concept of "glory" refers to "adoration and praise offered in worship." Christianity and Islam are in agreement that all glory belongs to God. None of God's creation is worthy of the adoration and praise that belongs to God alone. This appears to be part of the reason why God, himself, says in the Bible, "I will not yield my glory to another" (Isaiah 42:8).

Jesus and glory

If God will not yield His glory to another, then there is a verse in the Bible that needs explanation. In John 17:5 Jesus says, "And now, Father, glorify me in your presence with the glory I had with you before the world began."

From John 17:5 we learn several things about Jesus. First, Jesus prays to God the Father. Second, Jesus sees the Father as willing and able to confer glory upon him. Third, Jesus previously shared glory with the Father. Fourth, Jesus shared glory with the Father before the world began.

For those who have been taught that Jesus is a mere prophet, here is a simple question:

How can a mere prophet share glory with God?

It is clear from both the Qur'an and the Bible that God alone deserves all glory, and that God does not yield his glory to anyone. If Jesus previously shared glory with God the Father, and the glory was restored to Jesus by God the Father, is this not further evidence that Jesus is more than a prophet?

Jesus' condescension and exaltation

Jesus' prayer in John 17:5 is related to what the Apostle Paul writes in Philippians 2:6-8, where Jesus was said to be "in very nature God," shared "equality with God," yet took on "the very nature of a servant, being made in human likeness," and "humbled himself" and became "obedient to death...on a cross." The Philippians passage is thought by many scholars to be an early Christian hymn (i.e., written sometime before A.D. 62, the approximate date of Philippians). Whether or not it was a pre-Pauline hymn,[1] the clear teaching of the passages is that Jesus left the glory of heaven, as Jesus Himself says in John 17:5, took on human form, and died on a cross.

What follows this "condescension" of God the Son is his exaltation: "Therefore God exalted him to the highest place and gave him the name that is above every name, that at the name of Jesus every knee should bow, in heaven and on earth and under the earth and every tongue acknowledge that Jesus Christ is Lord, to the glory of God the Father" (Philippians 2:9-11). This is precisely the exaltation to glory that Jesus prays for in John 17:5, where Jesus asks the Father to restore the glory that he shared with the Father from eternity past.

The preceding verses hardly make sense if Jesus is a mere prophet. But what if Jesus is the eternal Son who shared glory with the Father from eternity past? What if he is the one who obediently came to earth as a human to die for the sins of the world, and who was exalted to his former position of glory at the right hand of God the Father? If these claims are true of Jesus, then the preceding verses make perfect sense. The conclusion, therefore, is that Jesus is more than a prophet.

PART TWO

WHO DID JESUS, HIS FOLLOWERS AND HIS ENEMIES SAY HE WAS?

CHAPTER TEN
What Jesus' Followers Said About Him

There are four biographies of the life and teachings of Jesus contained in the New Testament. These four are the canonical "Gospels," a term that means "good news." The Gospels were written by two disciples of Jesus (Matthew and John) a follower of Jesus who recorded the recollections of the Apostle Peter (Mark), and an investigative journalist (Luke).

In addition to the Gospels, nearly half of the New Testament was written by the Apostle Paul, who had his own personal encounter with the risen Lord on a road to Damascus (see Acts 9:1-9). These writers either knew Jesus personally, told the story of those who knew Jesus personally, or received information about Jesus from those who knew Him. In short, these writers were in the best position to hear and record Jesus' teachings, including teachings about Jesus' identity. To these followers of Jesus, was he more than a prophet? Here are the conclusions drawn from their accounts:

1. Jesus possessed the prerogatives of deity.

Previously this book presented evidence showing attributes belonging to God alone are ascribed to Jesus by his followers. These include Jesus as Creator (chapter one), receiving worship (chapter three), being the First and Last (chapter four), being prayed to (chapter five), being the final judge (chapter seven), and sharing God's glory (chapter nine). Both the Apostle John and the Apostle Paul claimed Jesus possessed attributes that belong only to God.

John says that Jesus is the creator of all things, writing, "Through him all things were made; without him nothing was made that has been made" (John 1:3) and "the world was made through him" (John 1:10). Paul writes in Colossians 1:16, "all things have been created through him and for him."

The claim that Jesus is the Creator also appears in Hebrews 1:2, where it says God appointed the Son to be heir of all things, and "through whom also he made the universe." "Creator" is a title that belongs exclusively to God, so from these verses we see that Jesus' followers understood that Jesus possessed the prerogatives that belong to God alone, implying that Jesus is God. In addition, the writer of the Hebrews makes clear that Jesus is to be worshiped (Hebrews 1:1-6).

Paul presents several claims to Jesus' pre-existence (e.g., Philippians 2:5-11) and asserts that Jesus will be the one who judges people's secrets (Romans 2:14-15). Finally, Paul writes that Jesus had pre-existing glory in heaven, and has been exalted to his former status (Philippians 2:5-11).

The foregoing passages are what the followers of Jesus concluded about him. These passages reveal who they believed he was by means of the attributes and prerogatives of deity they ascribed to him. These passages are separate from what his enemies said about him, and what Jesus said about himself, which will be covered in the following chapters.

2. Jesus was God in human form

John 1:1 states that the Word (Greek *Logos*) was "face to face" with God and was God. This being called the "Word" existed "in the beginning" (1:1) and "became flesh and made his dwelling among us" (John 1:14). This obvious reference to Jesus shows that he pre-existed as God before becoming a man.

In addition to the teaching in John chapter one that Jesus was God in human form, there is the great confession of Thomas in John 20:28 confirming that Jesus is God. After his crucifixion Jesus appeared to the disciples in a closed room when Thomas was absent. When Thomas later met up with the disciples they told him that Jesus had appeared, but Thomas was skeptical, and wanted to not only see for himself but also touch the crucifixion wounds before he would accept that Jesus had risen. Eight days later, when Thomas was present with the rest of the disciples, Jesus appeared again. Thomas, seeing Jesus and his wounds, said, "My Lord and my God" (John 20:28). This was a direct statement made to Jesus in the presence of the disciples, confirming Thomas' belief that Jesus was God in human form.

3. Jesus is the "only begotten God"

John 3:16 says that God loved the world by sending his "only begotten Son." The term "only begotten (Greek *monogenes*) can also have the meaning of "unique." Earlier in his Gospel, John writes," No one has ever seen God, but the one and only Son, who is himself God and is in closest relationship with the Father, has made him known" (John 1:18). Here, "one and only" is a translation of *monogenes*. More to the point, the verse says, "who is himself God." It is difficult to see how John could make it clearer that Jesus was more than a prophet. Some translations of John 1:18 read "only begotten God." However this verse is translated, the import is the same—Jesus is God.

4. Jesus is the "Great God and Savior"

In Titus 2:13 and 2 Peter 1:1 we find the expression "our God and Savior Jesus Christ" (Paul's reference in Titus adds the word "great" before "God"). The expression "God and Savior Jesus Christ" is properly understood as "God who is our Savior Jesus Christ," not as two separate persons. What is the evidence for this assertion? There is a particular construction in Greek that appears in these two verses, and the correct way to translate this construction was articulated by Granville Sharp in 1798.[1] Sharp explains that the proper translation is "God who is our Savior Jesus Christ," stating that when a clause has the construction found in Titus 2:13 and 2 Peter 1:1, the first noun ("God") is identified with the second noun ("Savior"), and refers to the same person. Thus, according to the Granville Sharp Rule, "God" and "Savior Jesus Christ" refer to the same person,

5. In Jesus dwells the fullness of Deity

Besides referring to Jesus as the creator (Colossians 1:16), and "great God and Savior" (Titus 2:13), the Apostle Paul also says, "in Christ all the fullness of the deity lives in bodily form" (Colossians 2:9). Some feel the need to marginalize Paul in order to escape his clear references to Jesus as being God. These people suggest that Paul was a "loose cannon" whose theology was suspect. Those who say this about Paul are tacitly admitting he referred to Jesus as God, but they try to wiggle out of Paul's identification of Jesus as God by questioning the accuracy of his theology.

Paul's own testimony refutes the notion that his views are suspect. In Galatians chapters one and two, Paul relays the account of his two visits to Jerusalem. He spent time with Peter and James during the first visit, and was joined by John the Apostle during the second visit. Paul had these "pillars" of the church examine his teachings. After scrutinizing Paul's doctrine, Paul says, "they added nothing to my message." This helps demonstrate that the New Testament is consistent in presenting God's truth through human writers, including Paul. Those, therefore, who reject Paul as a legitimate source of teaching about Jesus do so without any historical justification. It would be simpler for those who fault Paul's teachings to merely say they don't agree with him. Instead, they go to great lengths attempting to create a rift between Paul's teachings and that of Jesus, despite the fact that Paul's teachings about Jesus' divinity are consistent with Matthew, Mark, Luke, John and the writer to the Hebrews.

To summarize, Jesus' followers claimed that Jesus was God in human form, possessing the unique titles and attributes of divinity. Those who knew him best considered him to be more than a prophet.

CHAPTER ELEVEN
What Jesus' Enemies Said About Him

Historians attempt to arrive at what actually happened in the past by following certain criteria of historiography. If certain factors are present in an account, there is greater likelihood that the account is true. These criteria include multiple attestations (where other sources confirm the event) and the testimony of hostile witnesses, including enemies. Why is this so? Enemies do not typically embellish the stature of their foe, and instead are more likely to tell the unvarnished truth, whereas friends might provide a sanitized version of events.

In the case of Jesus, his enemies had a lot to say about the claims Jesus made in their presence. Their understanding of who he claimed to be is as powerful, if not more so, than the testimony of his followers. Thus, as a basic principle of historical analysis, the statements of Jesus' enemies must be considered in order to determine whether Jesus claimed to be merely a prophet.

1. He made Himself equal with God

In John chapter five, the Apostle John relays the account of Jesus healing a man who had been ill for 38 years. Certain Jews became aware that the man had been healed, but were upset because the healing had taken place on the Sabbath. The Jews found out from the man that it was Jesus that had healed him, which caused them to persecute Jesus for healing a man on the Sabbath (5:16). "In his defense Jesus said to them, 'My Father is always at his work to this very day, and I too am working'" (John 5:17). John then tells us, "For this reason they tried all the more to kill him; not only was he breaking the Sabbath, but he was even calling God his own Father, making himself equal with God" (John 5:28).

From the context it is clear that Jesus was doing more than saying God is the Father of all, because the Jews would have accepted that. Several places in the Old Testament God is called "Father" and the people are called his "children." In Isaiah 64:8 the prophet Isaiah writes, "You, LORD, are our Father." Deuteronomy 14:1 says, "You are the children of the LORD your God."

What did Jesus say that made him "equal with God" in the eyes of his enemies? The fact that he said God was his own Father, and that he partook of the same nature as his Father, making him equal with God the Father. The offense of Sabbath breaking paled in comparison to what the Jews now understood as blasphemy. Claiming equality with the Father was blasphemy unless the person making the claim shared the divine nature. Thus, Jesus' enemies rightly interpreted Jesus' words to mean that he was equal with God, a principle that the Apostle Paul elaborates on in Philippians 2:6, "Who, being in very nature God, did not consider equality with God something to be used to his own advantage."

2. He made Himself out to be God

In John chapter 10 Jesus was in the temple portico of Solomon when the Jews asked him to plainly tell them if he was the Christ (10:24). In response Jesus talks about his sheep, saying, "I give them eternal life" (John 10:28), and that the Father "has given them to me" (10:29), and that "I and the Father are one" (10:30).

That last remark, "I and the Father are one," induced his Jewish opponents to pick up stones to stone him (10:31). Jesus responds, "I have shown you many good words from the Father. For which of these do you stone me?" (10:32). The Jews replied, "We are not stoning you for any good work, but for blasphemy, because you, a mere man, claim to be God" (10:33). Thus, the Jews understood what Jesus was claiming—that he was more than a mere prophet—he was God.

3. He did things that only God can do

In the previously discussed account of Jesus forgiving the sins and healing the paralyzed man in the house in Capernaum (Matthew 9:2-9, etc.), the reaction of Jesus' enemies again helps confirm the identity of Jesus. The Jewish leaders who were present understood that Jesus was, personally, conferring forgiveness on the man. Their response to his statement to the man, "Friend, your sins are forgiven you," was "Who is this man who speaks blasphemies? Who can forgive sins, but God alone?" (Luke 5:21). From the reaction of those who were present, it was clear that Jesus did something that only God can do, namely forgive sins.

The Jews rightly recognized that a mere man or a mere prophet who claimed to forgive sins would be speaking blasphemies. However, it would not be blasphemy if the one doing the forgiving were God. Jesus implies this by telling those present that "the Son of Man has authority on earth to forgive sins" (Luke 5:24), after which he healed the paralytic as proof that he has spiritual authority to do what only God can do, namely forgive sins.

When taken as a whole, the picture of Jesus through the eyes of his enemies becomes clear. He made himself equal with God, he claimed to be God, and he did things that only God could do. In response to his enemies' accusations, Jesus never denied that he was equal with

God, never denied that he claimed to be God, and never denied that he could do things only God can do. If his enemies had been mistaken about his claims to deity, then Jesus missed several great opportunities to set the record straight. Instead, Jesus "doubles down" on his divinity by repeatedly emphasizing his unique relationship with the Father, with whom Jesus was "one." These are not the words of a mere prophet.

CHAPTER TWELVE
What Early Christians Said About Jesus

Some writers perpetuate the myth that Jesus was a mere man whose followers deified him at the Council of Nicea in the 4th century. For example, fiction writer Dan Brown writes, "Constantine… held a famous ecumenical gathering known as the Council of Nicaea… until that moment in history, Jesus as viewed by His followers was a mortal prophet . . . a great and powerful man, but a man nonetheless. A mortal…Jesus' establishment as 'the Son of God' was officially proposed and voted on by the Council of Nicaea."[1] The best way to refute such nonsense and establish the actual beliefs of the generations of Christians after the apostles is to examine their quotes. The following are excerpts that demonstrate what early Christians said and believed about Jesus.

1. Ignatius (A.D. 30-108)

Ignatius of Antioch was the third bishop of Antioch in Syria, and was a student of the Apostle John. He was arrested and taken to Rome where he suffered martyrdom in about the year 108 according to 4th century church historian Eusebius.[2] During his journey to Rome scholars accept that Ignatius wrote six letters to churches and a seventh to fellow-bishop Polycarp.

In his Letter to the Ephesians, 18:2, Ignatius wrote: "For our God, Jesus the Christ, was conceived in the womb by Mary." He also wrote "God appeared in the likeness of man" (Letter to the Ephesians, 19:3) and "There is only one Physician, of flesh and spirit, generate and ingenerate, God in man, true Life in death, Son of Man and Son of God…Jesus Christ our Lord" (Letter to the Ephesians, 7:2).

2. Irenaeus (A.D. 115-200)

Irenaeus was Bishop of Lugdunum in Gaul, modern Lyon in France. He heard the preaching of Polycarp, who was a pupil of the Apostle John.[3] Irenaeus' writings included a comprehensive refutation of Gnosticism, a 2nd century heresy that denied New Testament teachings about Jesus. Irenaeus especially targeted the teachings of Gnostic teacher Valentinus. In his best-known book, *Against Heresies*, X.1. Irenaeus wrote "…Christ Jesus, our Lord and God and Savior…."

3. Theophilus (A.D. 116-181)

Theophilus was a Patriarch of Antioch, Syria. His only extant work is his *Epistle to Autolycus*. In this epistle, II, xv, Theophilus writes, "In like manner also the three days which were before the luminaries, are types of the Trinity, of God, and His Word, and His wisdom." Thus, Theophilus provides the earliest extant reference to the Trinity (Greek *trias*).

4. Justin Martyr (A.D. 100-165)

Justin was a pagan philosopher who converted to Christianity, eventually starting a school in Rome. Among his pupils was Tatian, who would write the *Diatessaron* ("through the four"), a Gospel harmony. Justin wrote at least three apologetic treatises (*First Apology, Second Apology, Dialogue with Trypho*). In his *Dialogue with Trypho* 126, Justin wrote, "[Jesus] was God, Son of the only, unbegotten, unutterable God," and in his *First Apology*, chapter 63, wrote, "The Father of the universe has a Son, who also being the first begotten Word of God, is even God."

5. Tatian (A.D. 110-172)

Syrian by birth, Tatian wrote his *Diatessaron*, a harmony of the four Gospels that was used extensively in the Syrian church for several centuries. In Tatian's *Address to the Greeks*, 21, he writes, "...God was born in the form of man."

6. Melito (d. 190)

Melito was the Bishop of Sardis in Asia Minor (modern Turkey). Although most of his works have been lost, Melito is quoted by Jerome (quoting Tertullian) and others. His most famous work is *Apology* for Christianity to Marcus Aurelius, which Eusebius' *Chronicon* says was written ca 169-170.

Two quotes from Melito related to the divinity of Jesus: "He rose from the dead as God, being by nature God and man" (On the Passover, 8-9), and "Being God and likewise being perfect man, He gave positive indications of His two natures...He was the true God existing before the ages" (Fragment in Anastasius of Sinai's "The Guide" 13).

7. Tertullian (A.D. 145-230)

Tertullian was an early Christian apologist and prolific writer. He is the first Latin writer to use the term *trinitas*. Tertullian wrote, "Thus the connection of the Father in the Son, and of the Son in the Paraclete, produces three coherent Persons, who are yet distinct One from another. These three are one essence, not one Person, as it is said, 'I and the Father are One,' in respect to unity of substance, not singularity of number" (*Against Praxeas*, xxv).

Conclusion on Early Christians' View of Jesus

According to Muslim apologist Shabir Ally, "The idea that Jesus is God did not become part of Christian belief until after the Bible was written, and took many centuries to become part of the faith of Christians."[4] From the foregoing quotes dating from the time of the Apostles to the end of the 2nd century, Ally's conclusion is demonstrably false.

Hebrews 1:8 has God the Father saying, "But about the Son he says, 'Your throne, O God, will last for ever and ever.'" This verse is quoted by Justin Martyr (ca 150) in his *Dialogue with Trypho*, 56, to prove the deity of Christ. Thus, there is a continuum from the New Testament to the first generations of Christians after the apostles affirming that Jesus was God. Therefore the belief from Scripture that Jesus was more than a prophet, and was, in fact, God the Son, can be traced seamlessly from the time of the New Testament into the second century and beyond.

CHAPTER THIRTEEN
What Jesus Said About Himself

In addition to what Jesus' followers, enemies, and early Christians said about who he was, no investigation of the identity of Jesus would be complete without considering what he said about himself. There are many claims Jesus made about himself that both individually and cumulative provide a complete portrait of who he was. What did Jesus, the prophet, say about himself?

1. All things the Father has are His

Jesus said in John 16:15, "All that belongs to the Father is mine." Jesus had no hesitation to tell the world that he and the Father shared everything. No mere prophet could begin to make such a claim.

2. He can answer prayer

In John 14:13-14 Jesus said, "And I will do whatever you ask in my name, so that the Father may be glorified in the Son. You may ask me for anything in my name, and I will do it." The prerogative of answering prayer belongs to God, alone, so when Jesus promises that he will answer prayer, his identity becomes clear.

3. He identified Himself as God who spoke to Moses through the burning bush

In the Book of Exodus, Moses was pasturing a flock near Mount Horeb when God began to speak to Moses through a burning bush

(Exodus 3:1-4). God reveals Himself as the God of Abraham, Isaac and Jacob, and commissions Moses to deliver the children of Israel from Egyptian slavery and bring them to a Promised Land. Moses wants to know God's name or title so that he can tell the sons of Israel Who sent him. God then tells Moses, "I AM WHO I AM. This is what you are to say to the Israelites: 'I AM has sent me to you'" (Exodus 3:14).

When the Hebrew text of Exodus 3:14 (אֶהְיֶה אֲשֶׁר אֶהְיֶה) was translated into Greek in approximately 250 B.C., the Greek (transliterated into English) begins, *egō eimi ho ōn.*[1] This includes both the verb *eimi* ("I am") and the participle[2] *ho ōn* from the verb *eimi* ("I am"). When Jesus was telling the Jews that Abraham rejoiced to see his day (John 8:56), he was claiming to be the Coming One that would redeem humanity. When the Jews wondered how Jesus could have seen Abraham, Jesus replied, "Before Abraham was born, I am!" (John 8:58). John's Gospel quotes Jesus by using the exact same words (*egō eimi*) that begin the Greek translation of God's words to Moses in Exodus 3:14 where God begins to tell Moses his name. The reaction of the Jews to the words of Jesus is telling—"At this, they picked up stones to stone him" (John 8:59).

John 8:58 is such a compelling claim of deity by Jesus that one organization, Jehovah's Witnesses, intentionally mistranslated John 8:58 to obscure Jesus' claim to be the God who spoke to Moses out of the burning bush. The 1950 edition of the Jehovah's Witnesses' New World Translation rendered Jesus' words in John 8:58 as "Before Abraham came into existence, I have been." The footnote to John 8:58 in the New World Translation attempted to justify the "I have been" translation by stating, "properly rendered in the perfect indefinite tense."[3] It was pointed out to the Jehovah's Witnesses that there is no such thing as the "perfect indefinite tense" in Greek. The reference to the "perfect indefinite tense" was later removed by the Jehovah's Witnesses, although they continue to maintain a footnote arguing that Jesus' words are not the same as what God said to Moses in Exodus 3:14. Apparently, according to Jehovah's Witnesses, the claim "I have been before Abraham" is an offense the Jews considered worthy of stoning.

4. Jesus and the Father are one

In John chapter 10 Jesus was in the temple area called "Solomon's Porch" when the Jews asked him to tell them plainly if he was the Christ (10:24). Jesus, in response, talks about his sheep, saying, "I give them eternal life" (John 10:28), and that the Father "has given them to me" (10:29), adding, "I and the Father are one" (10:30).

That last remark, "I and the Father are one," resulted in his Jewish opponents picking up stones to stone him (10:31). Jesus responded, "I have shown you many good words from the Father. For which of these do you stone me?" (10:32). The Jews replied, "We are not stoning you for any good work, but for blasphemy, because you, a mere man, claim to be God" (10:33). Thus, the Jews understood what Jesus was claiming—that he was more than a mere prophet—he was God.

Jesus defused the situation by pointing out that it was not blasphemy for him to call himself "God's Son" (10:36), because in the Old Testament God's agents were referred to as "gods" (e.g., Psalm 82:6). But Jesus then said, "the Father is in me, and I in the Father," (10:38) which caused the Jews to again try to seize him because they understood his unique claim, "I and the Father are one," to mean that he shared the divine nature with the Father. To try and explain this away with "Jesus is only saying that he and the Father are one in purpose" is to deny what Jesus is clearly claiming, as evidenced by the reaction of those who were there. Jesus was one in purpose with the Father, just as he wanted his disciples to be one in purpose, but the oneness of Jesus with the Father was much more than that.

Some who teach that Jesus was a mere prophet question Christianity's understanding, and, apparently, the understanding of the Jews who heard Jesus' words, "I and the Father are One." For example, Muslim apologist Hussaini Yusuf Mabera writes, "Can a son be of the same essence and age with his father?"[4] According to Mabera, "If the oneness of Jesus with God makes Jesus Christ God, then the oneness of God, Jesus and the disciples would have made the disciples as Gods also" [sic].[5] He adds, "The Christians should understand that the oneness was just in love and purpose, and not in essence or knowledge."[6]

In order to maintain Mabera's view, one would have to disregard all the other passages where Jesus is called "God" and is said to possess divine prerogatives such as forgiving sins and being the Creator. But, regarding the John 10 passage, to maintain Mabera's position one would have to believe that it was a capital offense to the Jews to claim oneness in love and purpose with God. Immediately following Jesus' assertion, "I and the Father are one," "His Jewish opponents picked up stones to stone him" (John 10:31). The reader must decide whose understanding of Jesus' words is more credible—those who were present to hear the words in their context, or those, today, who are committed to explaining away all biblical references to Jesus' deity, no matter how tortured the explanation.

5. He is equal with God the Father

In John chapter five Jesus healed a chronically ill man on the Sabbath. The man was told by Jesus to "Get up! Pick up your mat and walk" (John 5:8), and the man obeyed. The religious Jews were incensed that the man was carrying his mat on the Sabbath, to them a violation of the Law (c.f., Jeremiah 21:17, ff, "This is what the LORD says: Be careful not to carry a load on the Sabbath day… Do not bring a load out of your houses or do any work on the Sabbath").

When the healed man was confronted, he told the Jews someone had healed him, but he did not know who it was. Later Jesus found the man in the temple and spoke to him, warning him not to sin (John 5:14). The man then told the Jews it was Jesus who had healed him, but rather than rejoice that a man had been healed, the Jews were incensed: "Because Jesus was doing these things on the Sabbath, the Jewish leaders began to persecute him" (John 5:16). Jesus responded by saying, "My Father is always at his work to this very day, and I too am working" (John 5:17). John then writes, "For this reason they tried all the more to kill him" because "not only was he breaking the Sabbath, but he was even calling God his own Father, making himself equal with God" (John 5:18).

The Jews understood that Jesus was making himself equal with God. John the Apostle, who wrote the account, was acutely aware of what the Jews understood Jesus to be saying, but makes no mention of the Jews' understanding being wrong.

In his response to the Jews who wanted to kill him, Jesus confirmed that he possesses the attributes of divinity. Jesus tells them that he takes his cues from the Father, and can do whatever the Father does (John 5:19). He also tells them that just as the Father raises the dead and gives life, so also the Son gives life "to whom he is pleased to give it" (John 5:21). Finally, Jesus says the Father has entrusted all judgment to the Son (5:22), and the Son is to be honored "just as they honor the Father" (5:23). Jesus summarizes his equality with God by saying the Father "has given him authority to judge because he is the Son of Man" (5:27).

The use of the term "Son of Man" is another reference to Jesus' divinity. Daniel the prophet makes reference to a "son of man" in chapter 7, verses 13-14: "In my vision at night I looked, and there before me was one like a son of man, coming with the clouds of heaven. He approached the Ancient of Days and was led into his presence. He was given authority, glory and sovereign power; all nations and peoples of every language worshiped him. His dominion is an everlasting dominion that will not pass away, and his kingdom is one that will never be destroyed." The "son of man coming with the clouds of heaven" was a seemingly divine figure who is in heaven with the "Ancient of Days."

When Jesus was being interrogated by the High Priest hours before his crucifixion, the High Priest asked, "Are you the Messiah, the Son of the Blessed One?" (Mark 14:61). Jesus replied, "I am. And you will see the Son of Man sitting at the right hand of the Mighty One and coming on the clouds of heaven" (Mark 14:62). Jesus' reference to the "Son of Man coming on the clouds of heaven" was a clear reference to Daniel 7:13-14. The reaction of the High Priest confirms this: "The high priest tore his clothes. 'Why do we need any more witnesses? You have heard the blasphemy. What do you think?' They all condemned him as worthy of death" (Mark 14:63-64). This passages shows that Jesus was crucified not for what he did, but for who he claimed to be.

6. If you've seen Jesus, you've seen the Father

In John chapter 14 Jesus says, "If you really know me, you will know my Father as well. From now on, you do know him and have seen him" (14:7). In response Philip says to Jesus, "Lord, show us the Father and that will be enough for us" (14:8). Jesus answered, "Don't you know me, Philip, even after I have been among you such a long time? Anyone who has seen me has seen the Father" (14:9). He continues, "Don't you believe that I am in the Father, and that the Father is in me? The words I say to you I do not speak on my own authority. Rather, it is the Father, living in me, who is doing his work. Believe me when I say that I am in the Father and the Father is in me" (14:10-11). These are not the claims of a mere prophet. No other prophet said the Father was in him and he in the Father.

Jesus claims that seeing him is seeing the Father because he is in the Father, and the Father is in him. How can God the Father, a person according to the Bible, be "in" Jesus? According to Jesus, during a conversation he had with a Samaritan woman at a well near the town of Sychar, "God is spirit" (John 4:24). Jesus later explained to his disciples what "spirit" is, saying, "a spirit does not have flesh and bones, as you see I have" (Luke 24:39). If God (whether the Father or the Son) is "spirit," then in order to manifest himself he would need to take on a form. That is what the Bible teaches happened at Bethlehem—God the Son took on human form through a virgin conception, and, despite being God, as both God and man he "grew in wisdom and stature" (Luke 2:52).

Being both human and divine, Jesus could hunger and thirst, he could gain knowledge, and his human body could be killed. This does not mean that God could be killed, a misconception often raised by those who have been taught Jesus is a mere prophet. But God the Son could experience death through his humanity, which he did on the cross, and Jesus' humanity had the same limitations as any other human, such as not knowing everything, and needing to rely on the Holy Spirit for guidance. Questions involving how Jesus could have any limitations if he were God are addressed later in this book.

7. Jesus deserves the same honor as the Father

Jesus said, "the Father judges no one, but has entrusted all judgment to the Son, that all may honor the Son just as they honor the Father. Whoever does not honor the Son does not honor the Father, who sent him" (John 5:22-23). In these verses Jesus makes it clear that he is to be honored in the same way that people honor the Father. What mere prophet claims to deserve the same honor that is due the Father? From these two verses alone it is plain to see that Jesus is more than a prophet. Instead, he is someone entitled to divine honor.

8. He will raise himself from the dead

In John chapter two, Jesus was in Jerusalem and saw the crass prof-iteering that was taking place in the temple area. There were money changers charging exorbitant rates to change foreign currency into the local currency so that pilgrims attending feasts in Jerusalem could have the proper means to make their offerings. There were also vendors sell-ing sheep and doves, sacrificial animals used at the feasts, at highly inflated prices. Jesus made a whip out of cords, drove all the animals out of the temple area and overturned the tables of the money chang-ers (John 2:15). The Jews asked, "What sign can you show us to prove your authority to do all this?" (John 2:18). Jesus answered, "Destroy this temple, and I will raise it again in three days" (John 2:19). The Jews were incredulous, saying, "It has taken forty-six years to build this temple, and you are going to raise it in three days?" John adds, "But the temple he had spoken of was his body" (John 2:20-21).

When a debate opponent once tried to disprove Jesus' deity, he asserted, "God raised Jesus from the dead" I agreed, because God the Father (see Galatians 1:1, etc.) and God the Son raised Jesus from the dead (John 2:19, 21, "Destroy this temple, and I will raise it again in three days…But the temple He had spoken of was His body"). What mere prophet ever claimed that he was going to raise himself from the dead? Since the Bible also says the Spirit raised Jesus from the dead (Romans 8:11, "And if the Spirit of him who raised Jesus from the dead is living in you."), according to the Scriptures, the answer to "Who raised Jesus from the dead?" is "God the Father, God the Son, and God the Holy Spirit."

Summary of What Jesus Said About Himself

The Bible says all things the Father has belong to Jesus. Jesus can answer prayer, He is the God who spoke to Moses out of the burning bush, he and the Father are one, he is equal with God the Father, deserves the same honor as the Father, if you've seen Jesus, you've seen the Father, and he raised Himself from the dead. Not even one of these claims Jesus made about himself could be true of a mere prophet. Both Christianity and Islam accept that Jesus was a prophet, but Christianity affirms that he was more than a prophet. Since Islam teaches that Jesus was a true prophet of God, then his words should be trusted. Jesus prophesied that he would be killed and be raised up on the third day (Matthew 16:21), and taught that he was the divine Son of God. If Jesus was a true prophet of God, then he ought to be believed, including his prophecies of his death and resurrection and his claims that he was the unique, divine Son of God, equal with God the Father.

PART THREE

QUESTIONS MUSLIMS ASK

CHAPTER FOURTEEN
If Jesus Is God, How Can He Have Limitations?

Both Christianity and Islam affirm that God is limitless and all-powerful. This is further defined in Christian thinking to mean that God can do anything he wants that is consistent with his nature. The "consistent with his nature" qualifier attaches because that there are some things that even a limitless, all-powerful God cannot do. For example, God cannot sin, because sin is not consistent with His nature. God cannot lie, because that, too, would be inconsistent with him being the Truth.

Limitations of Jesus

What is taught in Scripture is that Jesus was God incarnate, yet the person of Jesus had limitations. For example, Jesus did not know the day or hour when he was returning to earth. Jesus said, "But about that day or hour no one knows, not even the angels in heaven, nor the Son, but only the Father" (Mark 13:32). Mark relays the account where Jesus saw a fig tree in the distance, and went to see if it had any fruit. When he reached the tree he did not find any fruit "because it was not the season for figs" (Mark 11:13). Mark also tells us, "He could not do any miracles there, except lay his hands on a few sick people and heal them" (6:5). Luke tells us Jesus "grew in wisdom and stature, and in favor with God and man" (Luke 2:52), and the writer to the Hebrews says, "Son though he was, he learned obedience from what he suffered" (Hebrews 5:8). Finally, in Mark 5:25-30, a woman with a hemorrhage touched Jesus, and he felt healing power had gone out of him, but did not see who had touched him, so he asked, "Who touched me?" (5:31).

How can a limitless, all-powerful God have such limitations? The simple answer is because he was both God and man. As man Jesus could hunger (Mark 11:12) and thirst (John 19:28), could grow tired (John 4:6), and suffer (Luke 9:22). Ultimately, his body could die (John 19:30). As a man he had the same human limitations that all humans have. As God, he was all-powerful, limitless, all-knowing.

The Bible teaches that God the Son, the eternal Word, took on human flesh at Bethlehem. Jesus, then, had both a human nature and a divine nature. This union of God and man, called the *hypostatic union*, is difficult to fathom, and our understanding of how one person can have two natures is derived from what is taught in the Scriptures. Beyond what the Scriptures teach, namely that Jesus was both God and man, we must resort to conclusions based on inferences. For example, we are told that when God took on human form that Jesus "was made lower than the angels for a little while," (Hebrews 2:9). Paul explains this in Philippians 2:5ff, where he says Jesus "made himself nothing by taking the very nature of a servant, being made in human likeness" (2:7).

What does it mean, that Jesus "made himself nothing?" These words are the translation of the Greek verb *kenaō* that means "to empty." What, exactly, did God the Son empty himself of? Most Christian scholars say he emptied himself of his prerogative to inde-pendently exercise his relative divine attributes.[1] Jesus still possessed such attributes as omniscience and omnipotence, but only exercised those as the Father allowed. Thus, Jesus could have human limitations, such as not knowing it was not the season for figs, yet have the power to curse the tree when the Father directed or allowed him to do so.

Christians have always been interested in understanding how Jesus' humanity interacted with his deity. Clearly Jesus was aware from an early age that he was the Christ, and God was his Father in a unique way. When Jesus was twelve, after attending a feast, he stayed behind in Jerusalem, but his parents thought he had joined the caravan that was returning to Nazareth. They could not find him, so they returned to Jerusalem and three days later found Jesus in the temple court sitting among the teachers and asking questions. When his parents wondered why he had stayed behind, Jesus said, "Why were you searching for me? Didn't you know I had to be in my Father's house?" (Luke 2:49). Thus, Jesus knew he was God's Son and that God was his Father early on.

From numerous passages in the Bible it is clear that Jesus' mission was to do the will of the Father. The fact that God the Son carried out the will of God the Father does not negate the Son's deity. Jesus' limitations were due to his humanity and his emptying himself of the independent exercise of his divine prerogatives and relative attributes. Jesus willingly condescended to a position where the Father was greater than him, and Jesus lived his life in submission to the Father's will and by the leading of the Spirit.

Christianity affirms that Jesus and the Father, both being God, are co-equal in their divine essence, but are not the same in position. The Father has a pre-eminent position so that the Son is subordinate positionally to the Father, and the Son is pre-eminent over the Spirit, so that the Spirit is subordinate positionally to both the Father and the Son. The Father is greatest in position, not in nature. The Father, Jesus and the Spirit share the divine nature, being three persons within the one essence of God.

As can be seen from the discussion above, Jesus' limitations as the God-man are not only taught in Scripture, but should be expected if Jesus was, indeed, truly human. Unless Jesus had true humanity, his life on earth has little value as an example of how we can also be lead of the Spirit in obedience to the Father. Also, in order for Jesus to fulfill his purpose in becoming man, namely to "give his life as a ransom" (Matthew 20:28), he had to be able to die physically. As God the Son, Jesus could not die, but his divine nature could experience death through the physical death of his humanity.

The incarnation was a unique event,[2] and is best understood by what is clearly taught in Scripture, namely that Jesus was both God and man. Over the centuries some have tried to explain the incarnation that either denies the true humanity of Jesus, denies the true deity of Jesus, or both. It is risky to try and make Jesus fit our human understanding of his dual nature, and it must be remembered that there is a difference between not fully understanding how God could become man and denying that God became man. Those who say Jesus was merely a prophet are in the latter category, rejecting his deity and him being the Son in defiance of what Jesus said about himself. Anyone who holds Jesus in high esteem ought to accept what Jesus said about himself when investigating his true identity.

CHAPTER FIFTEEN
If Jesus Is God, How Can God Die?

Christianity diverges from the teachings of Islam on both the identity of Jesus, and his work. Regarding his identity, Christianity understands the Bible as affirming Jesus was God incarnate. As to his work, Christianity accepts his death and resurrection as historical facts. From numerous passages in the Bible Christians conclude that Jesus was more than a prophet, being God the Son. Christianity also finds, from the Bible, the teachings of the early church, and even a secular historian,[1] that Jesus died on a cross. Islam sees Jesus as a mere prophet, and claims, based on the Qur'an, that Jesus did not die. There is no real debate on this issue, since all biblical and historical evidence supports the fact that Jesus died on a cross. Whether Christian, agnostic or atheist, liberal or conservative, New Testament scholars are in agreement regarding the death of Jesus. Skeptical scholar John Dominic Crossan sums up the question of Jesus's death, writing, "That he was crucified is as sure as anything historical can ever be."[2]

Those who have been taught that Jesus was a mere prophet will have to decide whether to maintain the façade that Jesus was not crucified despite all historical evidence to the contrary. For those at least willing to consider the possibility that Jesus died, the question arises: If Jesus is God, and if Jesus died on a cross, how can God die? This is an important question, but the answer is not difficult, and relates to what was previously presented, namely how Jesus could be God given his limitations recorded in the Gospels.

Jesus Predicted His Death

First, a fact that should be important to both Christians and Muslims is that Jesus predicted over and over that he would die. For example, in Matthew 20:18-19 Jesus said, "We are going up to Jerusalem, and the Son of Man will be delivered over to the chief priests and the teachers of the law. They will condemn him to death and will hand him over to the Gentiles to be mocked and flogged and crucified. On the third day he will be raised to life!"[3] If Jesus was a prophet of God, then what he told the disciples ought to be believed.

Jesus Died

As Jesus was being crucified, he said, "'It is finished.' With that, he bowed his head and gave up his spirit" (John 19:30). Following Jesus' death, his Roman executioners did not want him to remain on the cross during the Sabbath, so they checked to see if Jesus was still alive. A spear was thrust into Jesus' side, and blood and water came out separate, convincing the executioners that he was dead, and they therefore did not need to break Jesus' legs to hasten his death (John 19:31-34). After his resurrection Jesus spoke to the Apostle John saying, "I am the Living One; I was dead, and now look, I am alive for ever and ever!" (Revelation 1:18). The above-referenced verses that confirm the fact that Jesus died are a small sampling of the numerous passages that reference his death on the cross.[4]

The Meaning of "Death" in the Bible

The answer to the question of how Jesus, as God, could die involves understanding the meaning of the term "death" in the Bible. "Death" in the Bible does not mean "cessation of existence." Instead, it means "separation." By way of illustration, physical death does not mean our spirit, the essence of who we are, ceases to exist. Physical death means the spirit leaves the body, and the body is no longer animate, yet the spirit lives on. Similarly, spiritual death is separation from God, not cessation of the existence of the spirit. In the case of Jesus, when he was crucified his human and divine spirit never ceased to exist, even when his spirit left his body (John 19:30). As the Epistle of James says, "the body without the spirit is dead," (James 2:26). The body "dies," in that it is no longer animated by the life force, i.e., the "spirit," but the spirit, separated from the body, continues to exist.

Spiritual Death

When Jesus died on the cross, he experienced physical death when his human spirit left his body. His body was no longer animate, separated from his life force, but his spirit continued to exist. Though Jesus was just one person, he had a human and a divine nature, being fully God and fully man. Whatever Jesus' human nature experienced, so, also, did his divine nature. Thus, at the time Jesus' humanity experienced physical death, he also bore the sins of the world, resulting in him experiencing separation from the Father, i.e., spiritual death. Through his humanity, Jesus' divine nature experienced spiritual separation (e.g., Matthew 27:46, "My God, my God, why have you forsaken me?"). At no point was there actual spiritual separation between the Father and Son, since God is a unity in essence. But God the Son could experience spiritual separation from the Father through his humanity, although Christian thinkers do not all agree on whether the divine nature is capable of experiencing death.[5]

In short, at no point did Jesus, as God, cease to exist. Instead, Jesus separated from his human body (i.e., physical "death") and, while bearing the sins of the world, experienced spiritual separation from the

Father through his humanity (i.e., spiritual death). However, never did the essence of God actually separate, and never did God the Son cease to exist.

Conclusion

Those who have been taught that Jesus was a mere prophet need to get past the biblically and historically unsupportable belief that Jesus never died. It is time to follow the lead of Sheikh Hussein, a top Shi'ite cleric in Damascus, Syria, who remarked to Christian apologist Ravi Zacharias, "Professor, maybe it's about time for us Muslims to stop asking if Jesus Christ died on a cross and to start asking why."[6] Orthodox Christianity has never taught that God ceased to exist when Jesus died on the cross. What Christianity affirms can bee seen in what the writer to the Hebrews wrote: "But we do see Jesus, who was made lower than the angels for a little while, now crowned with glory and honor because he suffered death, so that by the grace of God he might taste death for everyone" (Hebrews 2:9).

Whether we can fully comprehend it or not, the Bible says God the Son took on human flesh, and as one person with both a divine and human nature, "tasted" death for us. It is clear that if by "death" is meant "cease to exist" then God, the Son, did not die. But if we follow the biblical understanding of "death" as meaning "separation," then it can be seen that Jesus "tasted death" for us, experiencing separation from the body when he "gave up His spirit" on the cross, and experiencing separation from the Father when he said, "My God, my God, why have you forsaken me?" The reason God the Father went to such lengths that he would allow God the Son to taste death for us is because he "so loved the world" (John 3:16). The knowledge of this love allows us to believe in and serve God out of gratitude, not fear.

CHAPTER SIXTEEN
Did Jesus Say "I Am God, Worship Me"?

Some who have been taught that Jesus is a mere prophet are told to ask Christians, "Did Jesus ever say 'I am God. Worship me?'" Of course, the reply hoped for is, "No." But a "No" answer is misleading, because Jesus did claim to be God, and also received worship (e.g., Matthew 2:2, 11; 14:33; John 9:38). In fact, as discussed in chapter three of this book, the Father commanded the angels to worship Jesus (Hebrews 1:6).

The exact words requirement is a two-edged sword

Perhaps what the question "Did Jesus ever say, 'I am God'" really means is, "did Jesus ever use those exact words when referring to himself?" The answer, then, would be "No." But Jesus also never said, "I am not God. Don't worship me." If we demand exact words from Jesus before accepting a claim about him as being true, the result is that we would know very little about Jesus. For example, since Jesus never said he was (1) born of a virgin, (2) a carpenter, (3) a prophet (4) or from Galilee, are we to reject these well-established facts? These facts are accepted by Christians and Muslims without any requirement that Jesus himself claim them to be true, and especially without the need for Jesus to use exact words before the claim is accepted as true.

Demanding exact words from Jesus before accepting a claim about him is, therefore, inconsistent with the beliefs of Christians and Muslims about him. Further, such a demand is, frankly, dumb.

Rather than demanding that truth claims come from a particular person and said in a particular way before they are deemed true, a more reasonable way to determine what is true is to look at the totality of the evidence. When it comes to the question of whether Jesus is more than a prophet, we have already seen that Jesus possesses and exercises certain attributes that belong only to God, such as being the Creator, forgiving sins, receiving worship, being called "First and Last," receiving and answering prayer, raising himself from the dead, being the final Judge of the nations, calling himself the "Truth, and sharing glory with God the Father.

In addition, Jesus' followers referred to him as "God" (e.g., John 20:28), his enemies said he "made himself equal with God" (John 5:28), and "made himself out to be God" (John 10:33). Further, early Christians called him God (e.g., Ignatius of Antioch, Irenaeus, Bishop of Lyon). Finally, Jesus himself said all things the Father has are his (John 16:15), he can answer prayer (John 14:13-14), he identified himself as God who spoke to Moses out of the burning bush (John 8:58 cf Exodus 3:14), he and the Father are one (John 10:29), he is equal with the Father (John 5:16), if you've seen Jesus you've seen the Father (John 14:9), he deserves the same honor as the Father (John 5:22-23) and he will raise himself from the dead (John 2:19-21).

The cumulative case for the identity of Jesus overwhelmingly presents him as much more than a mere prophet. The Bible presents him as God the Son. Not only does Jesus receive worship during his earthly ministry, God the Father commands the angels to worship him (Hebrews 1:6). In light of the evidence, those who have been taught that Jesus is a mere prophet will either have to be abandoned that view or acknowledge that no amount of evidence will convince them to change their view.

The danger of traditions

It is not easy to go against traditions we were raised in, especially if there are good memories attached to those traditions, and the traditions have been celebrated by family and community for generations. But good memories are not a test of what is true. Just like Jesus' disciples who had to abandon many of their traditions in exchange for the truth, a true seeker of God will want to follow Jesus' teachings, even if it means going against traditions. Jesus warned the religious leaders of his time about this, saying, "you nullify the word of God for the sake of your tradition" (Matthew 15:6). He added, "These people honor me with their lips, but their hearts are far from me. They worship me in vain; their teachings are merely human rules" (Matthew 15:8-9).

If traditions are keeping anyone from acknowledging that Jesus is more than a prophet, it is time to abandon those traditions and follow what Jesus said. Jesus told us that it is possible to worship God in vain. To "worship God in spirit and in truth" (John 4:24) means leaving human rules behind, and following the truth God has revealed about himself and his plan. That plan includes the teachings of the Bible that God became flesh so that he might bear our sins. We must not let traditions nullify the word of God.

CHAPTER SEVENTEEN
Does the Old Testament Show that Jesus Is God?

The Bible nowhere tries to prove God exists. In fact, it says in more than one place, "the fool has said in his heart 'there is no God'" (e.g., Psalm 14:1, 53:1). The Bible starts out, "In the beginning God created the heavens and the earth" (Genesis 1:1).

Clues to understanding the nature of God

When Genesis 1:1 mentions "God," the word "God" is a translation of the Hebrew word *Elohim*. There is something unusual about the word *Elohim*. The word is a noun, but it is a grammatically singular noun with a plural masculine ending. The noun *Elohim* takes a singular verb. This unusual word may be a clue about the nature of God. Other cultures that existed at the time when Genesis 1:1 was written never used the plural *Elohim* in the way the Bible does. Instead, they used the simple singular *el*.[1]

There is also a covenant name for God used in the Old Testament. It is a name the Jews did not pronounce as a show of reverence. The covenant name for God consists of four consonants: YHWH. Depending on what vowels are inserted, the covenant name could be *Yahweh*, or *Yehowah*.[2] Most scholars today use *Yahweh* to refer to God's covenant name.

The God of Genesis

There are verses in Genesis that may also be further clues about God's nature. Genesis 1:26 reads, "Then God (*Elohim*) said, 'Let us make mankind in our image, in our likeness.'" Why use the plural pronoun "us?" Why use the plural possessive pronoun "our?" In addition, Genesis 3:22 reads, "The LORD God (*Yahweh Elohim*) said, 'Behold the man has become like one of us.'" Another plural pronoun used by God referring to himself. Finally, in Genesis 11:7, "God (*Yahweh*) said, 'Come let us go down there and confuse their language.'" Another plural pronoun used by God referring to himself.

These verses cannot refer to God talking to angels, since Genesis 1:26 says, "Let us make mankind in our image, in our likeness," and the next verse says, "So God created mankind in his own image, in the image of God he created them." Scholar Gleason Archer comments on Genesis 1:26, "The first person plural can hardly be a mere editorial or royal plural that refers to the speaker alone, for no such usage is demonstrable anywhere else in biblical Hebrew."[3] Thus, there is a plurality of persons in these verses.

Those who are invested in rejecting the biblical teaching that God has revealed himself in three persons typically will claim these uses of "us" and "our" are examples of "plural of majesty." The poetic device "plural of majesty" is claimed to be similar to the "editorial we" in which a person uses "we" to refer to himself or herself. An oft-cited example is the time an off-color joke was told in the presence of Queen Victoria, to which she replied, "we are not amused." In context, she was intending to speak on behalf of other ladies who were present and were also offended, hardly an actual example of "plurality of majesty." Thus, even presumed historical uses of plural of majesty are questionable. Is it possible that the Genesis references are the Hebraic use of plural of majesty? Absolutely no.

According to Hebrew scholars, there are no examples of the use of plural of majesty in the Bible.[4] This device was first used around the 4th century A.D., and was "a thing unknown to Moses and the prophets. Pharaoh, Nebuchadnezzar, David and all the other kings...speak in the singular, and not as modern kings in the plural. They do not say we, but I, command."[5] Anyone disputing the conclusions of these Hebrew scholars, namely that there is no "plural of majesty" used in the Bible, needs to come forward with credible evidence to the contrary.

The God of Isaiah

Isaiah the Prophet makes many references to God. Those that have a reference to Jesus include Isaiah 7:14 and 9:6.

Isaiah 7:14

Isaiah 7:14 says, "Therefore the Lord himself will give you a sign: The virgin will conceive and give birth to a son, and will call him Immanuel." On its face this verse looks like a reference to Jesus' virgin birth. However, those who find it problematic that a son would be called "Immanuel" ("God with us") argue that the Hebrew word translated "virgin" actually means "young woman." Although the Hebrew word *almah* can mean "young woman," there are three main reasons why Isaiah is referring to a "virgin."

First, the context. God tells Ahaz to ask for a sign from him, but Ahaz refuses, seeing it as "testing God." As a result, God says he is going to give a sign, but does not say he is giving it to Ahaz (i.e., "you" singular). Instead, when God says, "the Lord himself will give you a sign," the word "you" is plural, meaning it is a sign to the entire House of Israel. As such, what kind of sign would it be to the entire House of Israel that a young woman would conceive and bear a son? Such an everyday occurrence hardly constitutes a "sign."

Second, from the understanding of the Jews themselves. When the Jews translated the Hebrew Old Testament into Greek around 250 B.C. (the "Septuagint"), when they came to the Hebrew word *almah* in Isaiah 7:14, they translated it with the Greek word *parthenos*. The Greek word *parthenos* always means "virgin." Thus, the Jews themselves, 250 years before the birth of Jesus, saw Isaiah 7:14 as a prediction of a virgin birth.

Third, the New Testament links Isaiah 7:14 to Jesus' virgin conception. The angel Gabriel announced to Mary that she will conceive and bear a son. Mary was perplexed because she was a virgin, so Gabriel explained that the Holy Spirit would conceive the child in her womb, and he would be the Son of God (Luke 1:26-35). Matthew also confirms the virgin conception of Jesus. In Matthew 1:23 he quotes Isaiah 7:14 as being fulfilled in Jesus, writing, "The virgin will conceive and give birth to a son, and they will call him Immanuel" "(which means "God with us)."

Thus, the context, the Jews themselves, and the Gospel accounts all support Isaiah 7:14 as being a prophecy of Jesus' virgin birth, with the Gospels confirming that he will be "God with us."

Isaiah 9:6

In Isaiah 9:6 we read, "For to us a child is born, to us a son is given, and the government will be on his shoulders. And he will be called Wonderful Counselor, Mighty God, Everlasting Father, Prince of Peace." At the outset, what "son" throughout history has been called "Mighty God" (Hebrew *El Gibbor*) other than Jesus? Even Jehovah's Witnesses, an unorthodox religious group who teach that Jesus is a created being, consider Jesus to be "Mighty God," but not, "Almighty God."[6]

Trying to explain away Isaiah 9:6 as a reference to the divinity of Jesus leads some to quite fanciful conclusions. For example, one Muslim writer concludes that the "son" of Isaiah 9:6 is Solomon! One can only imagine Solomon's reaction upon being told he is the "Wonderful Counselor, Mighty God, Everlasting Father and Prince of Peace." The Muslim writer continues, "Solomon was…the everlasting spiritual father of his people…As for the title: 'Mighty God.' We know that prophet Isaiah [sic] was only speaking in a prophetic or figurative language. He does not mean that the son to be born will be creator of the universe or the Almighty. It was only a figure of Speech."[7]

The lack of consistency in this writer's explanation is apparent. When he wants "figurative language" to fit Solomon, it is stretched to fit (i.e., "everlasting spiritual father of his people"), but when the "figurative language" could never apply to Solomon (i.e., "creator of the universe or the Almighty") it is only a "figure of speech." This is a classic example of the Procrustean Bed in Greek mythology, where the rogue bandit Procrustes forced travelers to fit his bed by either cutting off their limbs if they were too tall, or stretching them if they were too short. Thus, a Procrustean Bed now refers to uniformity by arbitrary methods, as can be seen with the Muslim writer's inconsistent application of "figurative language" in Isaiah 9:6.

The title "Everlasting Father" (literally "Father of Eternity") may seem strange appended to one who is first called a "child" and a "son." But Jesus is the progenitor of a new generation, and the progenitor of eternity, and in that sense "father." As the Second Adam Jesus is the father of a new and everlasting family of the redeemed, caring for his people as a father would for his children. Although Jesus and God the Father are one (John 10:30), their oneness is in their shared divine essence, not oneness of their person. They are distinct persons within the essence of the one God, yet their attributes are the same. He who has seen Jesus has seen the Father because Jesus is "in the Father" and the Father "in" Jesus ((John 14:9-11).

Conclusion

The Old Testament gives several clues regarding the nature of God, using the plural "we" and "us" to refer to the divine essence. The Old Testament also includes direct references to a child becoming flesh who is "God with us" and "mighty God." These previews of the one God's identity provide a foundation for what is revealed in the New Testament, namely that God is a tri-unity. When it is understood that the Bible teaches this about Jesus, then he ought to be accepted as the person he claimed to be, God the Son, who took on human flesh so that he might bear our sins. As the evidence shows, in both the Old and New Testaments Jesus is presented as more than a prophet. He is presented as God the Son.

CHAPTER EIGHTEEN
Three Persons Called God, But One God?

God spoke of the complexity of his nature when he gave a comparison between human thoughts and his thoughts: "As the heavens are higher than the earth, so are my ways higher than your ways and my thoughts than your thoughts" (Isaiah 55:9).

General revelation

The Bible teaches that we can know, outwardly through the creation, the existence, power and creativity of God. Psalm 19:1 says, "the heavens declare the glory of God;" Romans 1:20 says, "For since the creation of the world God's invisible qualities—his eternal power and divine nature—have been clearly seen, being understood from what has been made, so that people are without excuse." We can also know of God's existence inwardly through our conscience. Romans 2:15 says, "They show that the requirements of the law are written on their hearts, their consciences also bearing witness."

The creation points to a divine Creator, and the moral law in our hearts points to a God who has put his law there. Creation and conscience are the two aspects of "general revelation," where God has made his glory, power and morality known. However, "general revelation" does not reveal who God is, who we are, or what his plan is. To know who God is and what his plan is requires "special revelation."

Special revelation

Special revelation includes truth God has revealed through prophets. The writer to the Hebrews confirms this, adding the identity of God's last and greatest revelation: "In the past God spoke to our ancestors through the prophets at many times and in various ways, but in these last days he has spoken to us by his Son, whom he appointed heir of all things, and through whom also he made the universe" (Hebrew 1:1-2). According to this passage, Jesus is God's ultimate revealer of truth. Just a few verses later God the Father tells the angels to worship God the Son (1:6), followed by the Father saying to the Son, "Your throne, O God, will last for ever and ever" (1:8).

Humanity has the choice of either accepting what God is like based on what God has revealed, or rejecting some or all of what he has revealed because it is either contrary to traditions or is too complex to understand. For example, the Bible clearly teaches the incarnation, that is, Jesus, the Word, became flesh (John 1:1, 14). We can either accept this lofty teaching, which is seen throughout the Old and New Testaments, or we can reject it because we cannot fathom how God can become man. On a practical level, if we waited until we fully understood a particular thing before accepting it as true, we might never flip on a light switch, since most people don't fully grasp the intricacies of electricity. Further, it was the end of the 20th century when the consensus of science finally answered the question of whether light is a wave or a particle, determining it was both. Not understanding light does not prevent us from flipping on the light switch and let the light illuminate a room.

The Trinity

The Bible teaches that there is one God (Deuteronomy 6:4, 1 Timothy 2:5), but there are also three persons called God (i.e., God the

Father, Galatians 1:1; God the Son, John 1:1, 14, 18; God the Holy Spirit, Acts 5:3-4, 13:2). For these truths to be compatible—namely there is one God but three persons called God—the three persons must equal the one God. As early church writer Tertullian explained (c. 180), there is one divine essence (Greek *ousia*) but three persons who share the one divine essence. Each person is fully God, and each person is eternal.

God's unity of essence and plurality of persons is often described as a "tri-unity," or "Trinity." It is merely an assertion based on what the Bible teaches, namely that there is one God and three persons who share the essence of the one God. Although the term "Trinity" is not used in the Bible, the concept is present throughout. For example, Jesus said, "go and make disciples of all nations, baptizing them in the name of the Father and of the Son and of the Holy Spirit." The Apostle Paul's benediction to the Corinthians says, "May the grace of the Lord Jesus Christ, and the love of God, and the fellowship of the Holy Spirit be with you all" (2 Corinthians 13:14). These passages present all three persons in one verse.

The error of rejecting the Trinity because the term is not found in the Bible

Some who teach that Jesus is merely a prophet argue that since the term "Trinity" is not used in the Bible, therefore it is a false concept. As has been previously shown, the Bible teaches there is only one God, yet there are three persons referred to as God. When the three separate persons (i.e., Father, Son, Holy Spirit") are mentioned in the same verse, the concept of God as a Trinity is clearly present. Just because the term "Trinity" is not used in the Bible does not negate the truth of the doctrine of the Trinity. Using this logic to reject the Trinity would mean that Muslims would have to reject *Tawhid* ("oneness of God" in Islam), because the word *Tawhid* is not found in the Qur'an.

A Muslim would rightly say that the concept of *Tawhid* is in the Qur'an, but that assertion is not qualitatively different from Christians saying the concept of the Trinity is found in the Bible. We would all do well to approach God on his terms, acknowledging that he has revealed himself in three persons, even though our finite minds cannot grasp the intricacies of how the Trinity functions.

CHAPTER NINETEEN
What the Qur'ran Says About the Bible

The Old Testament Scriptures were completed around the year 400 B.C. Jews call the first five books of the Old Testament the "Torah," which the Qur'an calls *Taurat*. The New Testament was written sometime between A.D. 40-95, and the first four books are called the Gospels. In the Qur'an the life and teachings of Jesus are referred to as the *Injil* ("Gospel").

The Qur'an ("recitation") consists of what Muhammad claimed were revelations he received from an angel. Although Muhammad at first questioned the source of these revelations, he eventually believed the angel was inspired by Allah. These revelations were memorized by Muhammad's followers, and portions were written down. The revelations were finally compiled into the Qur'an by Caliph Uthman about ten years after the death of Muhammad in A.D. 632.

One of the clearest differences between the Bible and the Qur'an is the number of sources behind each. The Old Testament was written by some 30 different authors, while the New Testament has nine different authors. The Qur'an consists entirely of what Muhammad claimed he received from an angel.

There is much confusion regarding what the Qur'an says about the Bible. Some Muslim apologists claim that differences between Islam and Christianity are a result of the Bible being corrupted, although the Qur'an never makes this claim. In order to clear up misconceptions, this chapter will refer to the actual text of the Qur'an rather than rumors about what it says. Verses from the Qur'an reveal Islam's actual view of the Torah and Gospel at the time of Muhammad. These verses from the Qur'an show that at the time of Muhammad the Torah and Gospel were considered to be the inspired and preserved words of Allah. The Qur'an not only teaches that the *Taurat* and *Injil* are authoritative for Jews and Christians, but also that Muhammad himself revered them and was ordered by Allah to consult them for guidance. Here are the main points the Qur'an makes about the Torah and the Gospel:

1. Allah's revelation to Muhammad confirms the Torah.

Sura 2:40-41:

"O Children of Israel...believe in what I reveal, confirming[1] the revelation which is with you."

The English word "confirming" in this verse is a translation from Arabic words that literally mean "between your hands," i.e., "in your presence." This is a reference to the Jews *at the time of Muhammad* having Allah's revelation that is with them (i.e., the Torah). There is no qualifier to suggest the Jews *used to have* Scripture, but it was now corrupted, or that it refers only to "basic truths still discernible in the Bible," as some Muslim apologists try to argue.[2] If the Torah had been corrupted, this would have been a golden opportunity for Allah to set the record straight, but there is not even a hint in this verse that the Torah had been corrupted.

2. Allah inspired the Torah and the Gospel as a guide to mankind.

Surah 3:3:

"It is He Who sent down to thee (step by step), in truth, the Book, confirming what went before it; and He sent down the Law (of Moses) and the Gospel (of Jesus) before this, as a guide to mankind...."

This Surah also refers to what Muhammad had "between his hands" at the time he received the revelation of the Qur'an. Muhammad had the Torah and Gospel, which the Qur'an says Allah sent down "as a guide to mankind." As Muhammad received this revelation from Allah the Torah and Gospel were "in his presence". Nothing in this verse even suggests that the Law and Gospel were no longer "a guide to mankind." It would be reasonable to expect that if the Law and Gospel had been corrupted by Muhammad's time that Allah would have clearly revealed this to Muhammad, yet nothing is said. Thus, the Qur'an gives every reason for Jews and Christians to justifiably rely on the Torah and Gospel as a guide from God.

3. There is no distinction between what Allah revealed to Abraham, Moses, and Jesus and between what Allah revealed to Muhammad.

Surah 3:84

"Say: 'We believe in Allah, and in what has been revealed to us and what was revealed to Abraham, Ishmael, Isaac, Jacob and the Tribes, and in (the Books) given to Moses, Jesus, and the Prophets, from their Lord; we make no distinction between one and another among them....'"

It is difficult to imagine how the Qur'an could be clearer in affirming the inspiration of the Torah and the Gospel. According to this verse the Torah and Gospel are on par with Allah's revelation to Muhammad. Since the Qur'an is believed by Islam to be inspired by God, then it logically follows that the Torah and Gospel are equally inspired by God, since "we make no distinction between one and another...."

4. No one can change Allah's words.

Surah 6:115 and Surah 18:27:

"...none can change His Words."

If Allah revealed the Torah and the Gospel the same way he revealed the Qur'an, then the Torah and the Gospel are the inspired words of Allah that cannot be changed. How, then, could the Torah or the Gospel be changed? By conjecturing that the Torah and Gospel have undergone corruption, does not the Muslim apologist open up the possibility, then, that the Qur'an could also have undergone corruption? These Surahs that affirm "none can change" Allah's words create a two-edged sword. If, in spite of these Surahs, Allah's words in the Torah and Gospel are subject to corruption, then one has to allow that the Qur'an is also subject to corruption. Islamic apologists cannot have it both ways.

5. Muhammad believed in the Torah that existed in the seventh century.

Sunan Abu Dawud 4449:[3]

"...They set out a cushion for the Messenger of Allah and he sat on it. Then he said, "Bring me the Torah." It was brought, and he took the cushion from beneath him and placed the Torah on it and said: "I believe in you and in the One Who revealed you."

This Hadith confirms that Muhammad believed in the Torah that was brought to him, and he showed his reverence for the Torah by setting it on the cushion he had been sitting on. In Islam Muhammad is the greatest interpreter of the Qur'an, and he clearly interprets the Qur'an as requiring him to believe in the Torah that he had in his possession in the seventh century. The text of the Torah has not changed since the seventh century, and the Dead Sea Scrolls confirm the accurate transmission of the Torah over the centuries. Thus, to rely on today's Torah is to rely on the text that Muhammad believed in.

6. Muhammad believed that the pure Gospel existed at his time.

Jami at-Tirmidhi 2653:

(Muhammad said) "The Torah and the Gospel are with the Jews and the Christians, but what do they avail of them?"

In this Hadith Muhammad had just said "knowledge" was going to be "taken from the people" until there was virtually nothing left. Ziyad bin Labid al-Ansari, once considered by Muhammad to be an expert in Islamic law,[4] wondered how this was possible, since the people possessed Allah's revelation to Muhammad by memorizing and reciting it. Muhammad's response makes clear that merely having the revelation preserved through memorizing and reciting was not enough. The Jews and Christians still had their revelation, yet they were not following it. The point is that having God's revelation is not the same as the people availing themselves of the revelation. There is an important parallel here. According to Muhammad, at his time the Torah and Gospel were preserved and available in a similar way that the revelations that later became the Qur'an were preserved and available. Muhammad's point was that Muslims, Jews and Christians were all in danger of losing their knowledge of God because they were not availing themselves of the revelations they had in their possession.

Muhammad's entire point in this Hadith is dependent on his belief that the Torah and Gospel were in the hands of Jews and Christians at the time he made his statements. He states, in present tense, "The Torah and the Gospel *are* with the Jews and the Christians." He does not state "The Torah and the Gospel *were* with the Jews and Christians. This is strong evidence that the entire, uncorrupted teachings of the Torah and Gospel were in the hands of Christians and Jews at the time of Muhammad.

7. The Qur'an demands that Christians judge by what Allah revealed in the Gospel.

Surah 5:47

"Let the People of the Gospel judge by what Allah hath revealed therein. If any do fail to judge by (the light of) what Allah hath revealed, they are (no better than) those who rebel."

Christians, according to the Qur'an, are not only justified in judging by the Gospel, but are condemned as no better than rebels if they don't judge by the Gospel. Islamic scholar Abdullah Saeed says concerning surah 5:47, "in verse Q5:47, for instance, Christians are commanded to judge according to what was revealed in *Injil*. Since this *ayah* is addressing Christians of the time of Prophet Muhammad, it must refer to the *Injil* that they possessed at that time, the early seventh century CE."[5]

Saeed confirms what Christians today tell Muslims who have been taught the myth that the Gospel has been corrupted. He states that the Gospel referenced in the Qur'an is the Gospel that existed at the time of Muhammad in the seventh century. Since the text of the Gospels that we have today is identical to the text of the Gospels that existed in the seventh century, then the Qur'an, by application, commands

Christians to judge by the Gospel we have today. In brief, there was no corruption of the Gospel by the time of Muhammad, and the Gospel of his day is the same as today.

8. If Christians and Jews do not judge by the Gospel and the Torah, they have nowhere to stand.

Surah 5:68

> "O People of the Book! Ye have no ground to stand upon unless ye stand fast by the Law, the Gospel, and all the Revelation that has come to you from your Lord."

This verse gives Jews and Christians a mandate to judge by their respective Books, and cites as the source of their revelations their "Lord." If the source of the Law and Gospel is God, and if Allah is telling Jews and Christians their only ground to stand upon is the Law and Gospel, it makes no sense that Allah would allow the their only ground to become corrupted. Further, the verse is in the present tense, "Ye *have* no ground to stand on unless ye stand fast by the Law, the Gospel...." At the time of Muhammad, the Law and Gospel had to exist for Allah's statement to make sense. Since the Law and Gospel have not changed since the time of Muhammad, Jews and Christians cannot be faulted for standing upon the Law and Gospel they have today.

9. When Muhammad was having doubts about his revelations, Allah commanded that he go ask Christians for confirmation.

Surah 10:94

> "If thou were in doubt [o Muhammad], as to what We have revealed unto thee, ask those who have been reading the Book from before thee...."

First, this verse shows the Qur'an's high regard for the Jewish and Christian Scriptures. It also shows that what is in the Book (i.e., the Bible) is so reliable that even Muhammad should ask Jews and Christians about any doubts he was having regarding Allah's revelations.

10. Islamic scholarship confirms that the Jewish and Christian Scriptures are very much the same today as they were at the time of Muhammad, and the Qur'an's reference to Torah and Gospel does not refer to some "pure" text that only existed at the time of Moses and Jesus.

Professor Abdullah Saeed writes:

Since the "authorized" scriptures of Jews and Christians remain very much today as they existed at the time of the Prophet, it is difficult to argue that the Qur'anic references to *Tawra*t and *Injil* were only to the "pure" *Tawrat* and *Injil* as existed at the time of Moses and Jesus, respectively. If the texts have remained more or less as they were in the seventh century CE, the reverence the Qur'an has shown them at the time should be retained even today. Many interpreters of the Qur'an, from Tabari to Râzï to Ibn Taymiyya and even Qutb, appear to be inclined to share this view. The wholesale dismissive attitude held by many Muslims in the modern period towards the scriptures of Judaism and Christianity do not seem have the support of either the Qur'an or the major figures of *tafsir*. Further research is required to explore the complexities associated with the doctrine of *tabrif* and the social, political and intellectual contexts in which this doctrine developed within Islam.[6]

The Illogic that the Law and Gospel have been Corrupted

It is commonly asserted by Muslim apologists that the reason the Bible does not support Islam is that the Bible has been corrupted. As set forth above, the Qur'an does not teach the Torah and Gospel have been corrupted. Instead, the Qur'an and the Hadith teach that the Torah and Gospel were inspired by Allah, were preserved until at least the time of Muhammad, and are authoritative for Jews and Christians.

Muslim apologists who maintain the unsupported view that the Torah and Gospel have been corrupted have the burden of proving their assertion. For example, in order to prove the Bible has been corrupted, Muslim apologists need to provide evidence that tells us:

When did the corruption occur?

Who corrupted it?

Where has it been corrupted (i.e., some parts or all parts)?

How does anyone know where the Bible can be trusted and where it has been corrupted?

Why would Jews and Christians be told in the Qur'an to stand upon the Law and Gospel if it had been corrupted?

How is a corrupt Book a guide to all mankind?

The evidence shows that those who simply claim the Bible has been corrupted do so in order to avoid the conclusion that the Law and Gospel, which the Qur'an says were inspired by God, contradict the Qur'an and Islamic beliefs. For example, as has been shown in previous chapters herein, the Gospels present Jesus as God. Rather than acknowledge a contradiction between Christianity and Islam, the Muslim apologist either tries to explain away the numerous passages that ascribe deity to Jesus, or else dismisses the Gospels as "corrupt" without any evidence. These approaches are examples of "confirmation bias," where no facts are allowed that contradict a belief and any arguments that support a belief are accepted uncritically. This is similar to the account of a skeptic who questioned the resurrection of Jesus. The skeptic was asked, "If I could prove to you beyond any doubt that Jesus rose from the dead, would you believe?" The skeptic's answer was, "No." The skeptic's response revealed that the problem was not with his mind, but with his will. It was not a case of "I can't believe." It was a matter of "I choose not to believe." People are free to believe in spite of contrary evidence. However, one who does so is not exercising reasonable faith. Believing in spite of the evidence is, instead, *credulity*.

Conclusion

The Qur'an says it confirms the Torah, and that Allah inspired the Torah and the Gospel as guides to mankind. The Qur'an says there is no distinction between the revelations in the Qur'an and those in the Torah and Gospel. In addition to the Qur'an teaching the inspiration of the Torah and Gospel, it also teaches their preservation. Muhammad believed that the Torah existed during his time, and the Qur'an makes it clear that no one can change the words of Allah. Further, the Qur'an teaches the authority of the Torah and Gospel, demanding that Christians judge by the Gospel, and stating that Jews and Christians have no ground to stand upon if they don't stand upon the Torah and the Gospel.

Together these teachings from the Qur'an and the Hadith give Christians every right to follow the Gospel, and there is no mention in the Qur'an of any corruption of the Gospel that would abrogate the reliability of the Gospel as a revelation from God. Finally, according to the Qur'an, Allah himself told Muhammad to ask Christians about his revelations at a time that he was having doubts because they had been reading the Gospel.

Therefore, in light of the foregoing, not only does Christianity teach that Scripture is "God-breathed" (2 Timothy 3:16) and profitable for doctrine, but the Qur'an also teaches that the Gospel is a revelation from God, inspired, preserved and authoritative for Christians to follow.

CHAPTER TWENTY
If Jesus Is More Than a Prophet

This book intends to demonstrate by clear and convincing evidence that the Bible teaches Jesus was more than a mere prophet—he was God, the Son, a separate person within the essence of the one God. From Genesis to Revelation there are clues, inferences and direct statements indicating Jesus shares the divine nature, being ascribed the attributes of deity that no human prophet could ever claim.

The cumulative case for Jesus being God is compelling. Thus, it creates a dilemma for those who have been taught that Jesus is a mere prophet. To deny Jesus' deity is to reject Jesus as a prophet, because he made claims to deity, as did his followers, his enemies, and early Christian writers. So, what if someone reading this book now realizes that he was more than a prophet?

First, it means that God has opened a person's eyes to a new and fuller understanding of what he has revealed.

Second, it means that it is time for Jesus to be accepted as who he claimed to be. This includes him being:

1. The only way to God the Father (John 14:6, "No one comes to the Father except through me.").

2. The one who gave his life for us (Matthew 20:28, "the Son of

Man did not come to be served, but to serve, and to give his life as a ransom for many.")

3. Crucified, buried and raised from the dead (Matthew 16:21, "From that time on Jesus began to explain to his disciples that he must go to Jerusalem and suffer many things at the hands of the elders, the chief priests and the teachers of the law, and that he must be killed and on the third day be raised to life.")

4. The one we must believe in to be forgiven of sins (John 8:24, "I told you that you would die in your sins; if you do not believe that I am he, you will indeed die in your sins.")

5. The one who offers life (John 10:10, "I have come that they may have life")

6. The one whom the Scriptures are about (John 5:39, "You study the Scriptures diligently because you think that in them you have eternal life. These are the very Scriptures that testify about me")

7. The one who exposes errors about himself and the Father (Matthew 22:29, "Jesus replied, "You are in error because you do not know the Scriptures or the power of God."

Third, it means leaving behind traditions and beliefs that are contrary to what Jesus taught (Mark 7:8-9. "You have let go of the commands of God and are holding on to human traditions." And he continued, "You have a fine way of setting aside the commands of God in order to observe your own traditions."). When we are presented with truth that reveals a different path than the one we had previously been taught, would not God want us to follow the truth wherever it leads? Yes, if we believe that all truth is God's truth.

There may be consequences to leaving behind traditions that are in conflict to what Jesus taught. These consequences might include being misunderstood and falsely condemning for discovering who Jesus truly is. Following the truth might lead to being ostracized by friends and even family. It might even lead to physical danger. Jesus anticipated this for his followers, saying, "those of you who do not give up everything you have cannot be my disciples" (Luke 14:33). Are we willing to surrender traditions that deny the truth Jesus taught? This may be difficult for those who have spent their whole lives embracing traditions they were told were from God, only to find out the traditions conflicted with God's truth. Jesus makes it clear that we have to decide whether we are with him or not. He said in Matthew 12:30, "Whoever is not with me is against me."

Decision time

Those who have been taught Jesus was a mere prophet have to make a choice. Either continue to embrace traditions that deny what Jesus, the Son of God, clearly said, or move beyond those traditions and teachings, and embrace Jesus' words regarding who he is and what he has done. Jesus said we have a responsibility to act upon the truth we have been given (Luke 12:48, "From everyone who has been given much, much will be demanded; and from the one who has been entrusted with much, much more will be asked."). There is no better time than now to act upon what Jesus said. The Bible says,

> If you declare with your mouth, "Jesus is Lord," and believe in your heart that God raised him from the dead, you will be saved. For it is with your heart that you believe and are justified, and it is with your mouth that you profess your faith and are saved. As Scripture says, "Anyone who believes in him will never be put to shame" (Romans 10:9-11).

This book presents compelling evidence that God the Father created the world through God the Son. God the Son took on human flesh, and in concert with the will of the Father, lived a sinless life, died on a cross for the sins of the world, and rose from the dead as proof that he was the Promised One. According to Jesus, if we put our faith in him, trusting that he bore our sins on the cross, we will be saved. Those who trust him are promised eternal life with him in heaven (John 3:16, "For God so loved the world that he gave his one and only Son, that whoever believes in him shall not perish but have eternal life.")

Jesus offers his gift of eternal life freely to all who place their trust in him. His gift cannot be earned, since we could never do enough to merit the gift of eternal life. He offers it without cost, because he already paid the price by dying for our sins. Thus, by believing in him, you receive him as Lord and Savoir, and become a child of God (John 1:12-13, "to all who did receive him, to those who believed in his name, he gave the right to become children of God--children born not of natural descent, nor of human decision or a husband's will, but born of God."). Trust him now for your salvation, and study his Word, the Bible, for direction in you life. This is God's will for you and for me. May God give us all the courage to follow his truth.

APPENDIX ONE
Summary of God's Attributes

Islam and Christianity agree that the following attributes belong only to God:

Qur'an	Bible
1. God is the Creator of the universe	
Surah 42:11	Genesis 1:1
2. Only God forgives sins	
Surah 3:135	Isaiah 43:25
3. Only God is to be worshipped	
Surah 17:22, 23	Exodus 20:3,5
4. God is the First and the Last	
Surah 57:1, 3	Isaiah 44:6
5. God receives and answers prayer	
Surah 40:60	Psalm 50:15
6. Only God can give life and raise the dead	
Surah 22:7	1 Samuel 2:5
7. God is the final Judge of the nations	
Surah 22:56-57	Psalm 96:13

8. God is the Truth

   Surah 10:82   Psalm 31:5

9. God does not share His glory

   Surah 57:1   Isaiah 42:8

Yet the Bible also teaches that Jesus possesses the following attributes:

<u>Bible</u>

1.	Creator of the universe	John 1:3; Colossians 1:15; Hebrew 1:2;
2.	Forgives sins	Matthew 9:2-9
3.	Is Worshipped	Matthew 14:33; 28:9; John 9:38; Heb. 1:6;
4.	First and the Last	Revelation 1:17; 22:13
5.	Receives and answers prayer	John 14:13-14; Acts 7:59; 1 Corinthians 1:2
6.	Gives life	John 2:19-21; 5:21; 11:25-26
7.	Is the final Judge	Matthew 25:31-32; John 5:22; Rom. 2:16
8.	Is the Truth	John 14:6
9.	Shares glory with the Father	John 17:5

According to the Bible, all of the above-referenced divine prerogatives are attributed to Jesus. How, then, can Jesus be a mere prophet if prerogatives of deity are ascribed to him? How could a mere man, even one uniquely born of a virgin, possess such attributes? Could Jesus have wrongly usurped such divine attributes as judging the nations and receiving worship? No, because we read that God the Father has entrusted Jesus with all judgment (John 5:22), and God the Father tells the angels to worship Jesus (Hebrews 1:6). Thus, God the Father acknowledges Jesus' legitimate possession of divine attributes.

Since there cannot be two "Firsts" and two "Lasts," the fact that both the Qur'an and the Bible call God the "First and the Last" is problematic for those who have been taught that Jesus is a mere prophet, since Jesus is called the "First and the Last" (Revelation 1:17, 22:13). There is simply no way to wiggle out of the conclusion that a title uniquely ascribed to God is also ascribed to Jesus. If Jesus were a mere prophet, this ascription would be blasphemy. But if Jesus is more than a prophet, that is, God in the flesh, then he could properly be the First and the Last. This does not address *how* God became man, and how the divine nature interacted with the human nature of Jesus. But it does resolve the question of *whether* God became man. Indeed, he did, as demonstrated by the divine attributes ascribed to Jesus that no mere prophet could claim or possess.

The only rational conclusion from examining the divine attributes that are ascribed to Jesus is that he is entitled to those attributes and possesses them because he is God, the Son. No man, and no mere prophet is even remotely worthy of even one of these many divine prerogatives. Islam and Christianity agree that to ascribe these prerogatives to one who is not God is blasphemy. Since there is no way to avoid the conclusion that Jesus possesses divine prerogatives, the logic is quite compelling—Jesus is God.

APPENDIX TWO
The Gospel of Barnabas

The Canonical Gospels of Matthew, Mark, Luke and John are the only authentic biographies of Jesus from the 1st century. These Gospels were written by either eyewitnesses to the life of Jesus, or by writers who recorded the accounts of eyewitnesses.[1] 2nd century church leaders Papius (ca 110) and Irenaeus (ca 170) confirm the Gospels were written by Matthew, Mark, Luke and John. There are no traditions for anyone else writing the Gospels.

Sometime in the early-to-mid 2nd century certain unknown people began writing fictional accounts of the life of Jesus. In order to have their stories taken seriously, most of these writings claimed to be written by people mentioned in the New Testament such as Thomas, Philip and even Judas Iscariot. Many of these spurious "gospels" were written from the perspective of the cult of Gnosticism.[2] Others were written as pious fiction in efforts to provide Christians with entertaining reading material as an alternative to the salacious secular novels that were available.

Lost Gospels?

Sometimes these fanciful stories of the life of Jesus are called "lost gospels." In fact, like the breakfast cereal "Grape Nuts" which is neither grapes nor nuts, the "lost gospels" are neither lost nor are they Gospels. Some of these "lost gospels" were known in the 2nd through 4th centuries, but eventually discarded. Some have been recovered in the past 150 years, found in garbage dumps along with other Gnostic writings. These "lost gospels" add not a single verifiable new fact to the life and teachings of Jesus.[3] However, the mere idea that there are "lost gospels" that might contain suppressed truth about Jesus has become the basis for sensational claims by non-scholars in order to sell books or promote television specials about Jesus. Scholars place them in the category of *pseudepigrapha,* that is, "false writings" (or, "forgeries"). Sometimes these spurious writings are called *apocrypha,* meaning "hidden" or "esoteric" as opposed to *canonical* ("standard").

14th Century *Gospel of Barnabas*

Of all the so-called "lost gospels," one of the least deserving of attention is a 14th century Italian manuscript known as the *Gospel of Barnabas.* It would not even be discussed other than in esoteric books that catalogue pseudepigrapha, except that Muslim polemicists use it to support certain claims of Islam. The so-called *Gospel of Barnabas* begins by claiming it was written by Barnabas, an apostle of Jesus, who is said to be one of Jesus' twelve apostles.[4] Such a statement is not a good start for a writing that is apparently trying to present itself as being true, since Barnabas was not one of the twelve apostles. One thinks of the remark attributed to Mark Twain, of a man "born ignorant, and going down hill ever since." The *Gospel of Barnabas* starts out amazingly ignorant of the facts of the Gospels, only to get worse. For example, in the Prologue to the *Gospel of Barnabas,* right after Barnabas is called "apostle of Jesus the Nazarene," it says Jesus is "called Christ." The term "Christ" is the Greek equivalent of the Hebrew "Messiah," and both words mean "anointed one." However, the *Gospel of Barnabas* later has Jesus saying he is *not* the Messiah (Chapter 42) because, spoiler alert, Muhammad is the Messiah! (Chapter 97). Before addressing more of the glaring problems with the 14th century *Gospel of Barnabas,* a little background is called for.

Epistle of Barnabas

First, the spurious *Gospel of Barnabas* is entirely different from the *Epistle of Barnabas*, a 21-chapter epistle written in Greek and preserved completely in *Codex Sinaiticus* (ca 325) following the twenty-seven canonical New Testament books. The epistle is cited in the late 2nd century by Clement of Alexandria and early 3rd century by Origen. However, 4th century church historian Eusebius placed the *Epistle of Barnabas* in the category of *antilegomena* ("spoken against," i.e., disputed). The consensus today is that Paul's companion Barnabas mentioned in the Book of Acts was not the author. Instead, it is held that someone claiming to be Barnabas wrote the letter in the early 2nd century.

Acts of Barnabas

A 5th century pseudepigraphon entitled *Acts of Barnabas* exists that claims to be written by John Mark, Paul's traveling companion. No one seriously contends that this work is authentic, as it shows 5th century concerns involving the Church of Cyprus.

Gospel of Barnabas in Church History

A 6th century Latin document, attributed to Gelasius,[5] bishop of Rome 492-496, contains various lists of writings, including the New Testament canon and New Testament apocrypha. In the section dealing with the apocrypha, ("the books that are to be rejected") the Gelasian document lists several "gospels," including "Gospel under the name of Barnabas." The text of this "gospel" is unknown.

In the early18th century John Toland provides the first reference to a medieval *Gospel of Barnabas* written in Italian. In 1709 Toland borrowed a copy of the Italian manuscript and determined it was written in the early 15th century.[6] Toland, who was the first to write about the manuscript, considered the *Gospel of Barnabas* to be a forgery.[7] About 20 years later Arabic scholar George Sale mentions a Spanish version of the *Gospel of Barnabas*. Sale's quotes from the Spanish version agree with Toland's Italian copy. Sale determined the Spanish copy was made by "Mostafa de Aranda, a Moslem of Aragon"[8] from an Italian copy stolen from the library of Pope Sixtus V (1585-90).[9] The Spanish manuscript, believed to be from the 16th century is now lost, but a portion of the text exists in an 18th century copy.

The first English translation of the Italian *Gospel of Barnabas* was made in 1907 by Lonsdale and Laura Ragg, and in the introduction the translators provide substantial internal and external evidence demonstrating that the *Gospel of Barnabas* is a medieval forgery.[10] Later translations of the *Gospel of Barnabas* into Arabic and Urdu omit the introduction. The medieval *Gospel of Barnabas* is the length of the four canonical Gospels combined, and is divided into 222 short "Chapters."

Why the *Gospel of Barnabas* is a Medieval Forgery

Irrefutable evidence demonstrates the *Gospel of Barnabas* is a 14th century forgery created with the intent of deceiving readers into believing that teachings in the Qur'an come from 1st century accounts of an apostle. It is patently obvious that a Muslim polemicist conflated authentic Gospel accounts and created new sayings of Jesus to support the peculiar teachings of Islam. Ironically, the *Gospel of Barnabas* not only contradicts the teachings of the canonical Gospels, but it also directly contradicts teachings found in the Qur'an. Evidence that proves the *Gospel of Barnabas* is a medieval forgery is overwhelming. The examples are numerous, and the following are a mere sampling:

1. *Gospel of Barnabas* rewrites Gospel accounts to harmonize with the Qur'an.

Jesus denies he is the Messiah

Although the Qur'an acknowledges Jesus as Messiah[11] the *Gospel of Barnabas* has Jesus denying that he is the Messiah (Chapter 42)[12] and reserves the title "Messiah" for Muhammad (Chapter 97).

Jesus denies he is the Son of God

In Matthew chapter 16 Jesus asks his disciples who they say he is, and Peter responds, "You are the Messiah, the Son of the living God." The 7th century Qur'an states repeatedly that Allah has no Son (e.g., Surah 2:116). Since denying Jesus is the Son of God contradicts the much older New Testament Gospels, how can the Qur'an be correct? Along comes the *Gospel of Barnabas*. In its version of the account where Peter acknowledges Jesus is the Son of God, instead of blessing Peter, as he does in the biblical account, Jesus is angry and rebukes Peter, saying, "'Begone and depart from me, because thou art the devil and seekest to cause me offence!' And he threatened the eleven, saying: 'Woe to you if ye believe this, for I have won from God a great curse against those who believe this'" (Chapter 70).

Judas Iscariot dies in Jesus' place

According to the *Gospel of Barnabas* Chapter 216, God changed Judas to look and sound like Jesus, so that even the disciples did not know it was Judas. Then the soldiers arrested Judas, thinking him to be Jesus. Judas then tells the high priest that he is not Jesus, but neither the high priest, Pilate or Herod believe him, and Judas is then crucified instead of Jesus (Chapter 217). This re-telling of the actual Gospel accounts is consistent with the Qur'an's denial that Jesus was crucified (Surah 4:157, "they killed him not, nor crucified him, but so it was made to appear to them").

Many more examples exist of the *Gospel of Barnabas'* transparent attempts to re-write the life of Jesus to harmonize it with the Qur'an. In addition to these glaring attempts to turn Muslim myth into truth, the *Gospel of Barnabas* also contains many anachronistic passages that betray it as a medieval forgery.

2. Anachronisms that reveal the *Gospel of Barnabas* is a medieval forgery

Quotations from Dante's Inferno

Dante Alighieri wrote a poem in the early 14th century entitled *Divine Comedy*. In it Dante describes a journey through hell, purgatory and heaven. One of the phrases that appears in the *Gospel of Barnabas* in several places is "false and lying gods"[13] (Chapters 23, 78, 217). This phrase is a direct quote from *Divine Comedy* 1.72, and nowhere does it appear in either the Bible or the Qur'an.

The year of Jubilee

According to Leviticus 25:11, every 50th year was to be a "Year of Jubilee" in which debts were canceled and slaves could go free. Pope Boniface VIII, in the year 1300, established a "Holy Year," resembling the Year of Jubilee, as a centenary (i.e., every 100 years) observance. In 1342 Clement VI reduced the interval back to 50 years, and in 1470 Paul II further reduced it to 25 years.[14] In the *Gospel of Barnabas*, Chapter 82, Jesus says:

> I am indeed sent to the house of Israel as a prophet of salvation; but after me shall come the Messiah, sent of God to all the world; for whom God hath made the world. And then through all the world will God be worshipped, and mercy received, insomuch that the year of jubilee, which]now cometh every hundred years, shall by the Messiah be reduced to every year in every place.

This paragraph exposes the writer of the *Gospel of Barnabas* as being aware of Pope Boniface VIII's decree from the 14th century, while anachronistically placing the Year of Jubilee nearly 1,300 years earlier in an utterance by Jesus. This is irrefutable evidence that the *Gospel of Barnabas* could not have been written prior to the year 1300.

Quotations from the Latin Vulgate

Jerome translated the Old and New Testaments into Latin in around 390. All biblical quotations found in the *Gospel of Barnabas* are taken from the *Latin Vulgate.* It is difficult to support the authenticity of a purported 1st century document like the *Gospel of Barnabas* when it quotes a text that did not exist until the late 4th century.

Three wise men

In the authentic Gospel of Matthew, wise men ("Magi") come from the east looking fore the King of the Jews. When they found baby Jesus "they bowed down and worshiped him. Then they opened their treasures and presented him with gifts of gold, frankincense and myrrh" (Matthew 2:11). Because of the three gifts, by the 5th century Western Church tradition determined that there were three wise men, and even provided their supposed names.[15] However, in Eastern Church tradition the Magi number twelve. The *Gospel of Barnabas,* apparently written in the West, adopts the extra-biblical tradition of three wise men (Chapter 6).

3. Factual errors and absurdities

Misplacing Nazareth

Anyone who has been to Israel and has passed through Nazareth knows that Nazareth is still a ways away from the Sea of Galilee (around 25 kilometers, 16 miles "as the crow flies"). In Chapter 20 of the *Gospel of Barnabas* we read, "Jesus went to the sea of Galilee, and having embarked in a ship sailed to his city of Nazareth." Since the Sea of Galilee is only 13 miles long, it is difficult to see how Jesus could have sailed on a thirteen-mile long lake and arrived at a town 16 miles away from the water. Clearly, the *Gospel of Barnabas* was written by someone with a total ignorance of the geography of Palestine.

Misplacing Pontius Pilate

Secular historian Cornelius Tacitus confirms the Gospel account that Jesus was crucified during the reign of Roman Prefect Pontius Pilate. Roman histories confirm Pilate's rule in the province of Judea was from 26 to 36. The *Gospel of Barnabas,* Chapter 3, has Pilate as governor at the time Caesar Augustus' decree that lead Mary and Joseph to Bethlehem, which most scholars set around 4 B.C. Thus, the *Gospel of Barnabas* shows a total lack of understanding of the chronology of people and events in Judea at the time of Jesus.

Misplacing the Pharisees

The Pharisees were a separatist group of religious, legalistic Jews that emerged in the early 3rd century B.C. or late 2nd century B.C., just prior to the 2nd century Maccabean revolt. The Pharisees developed as a response to many Jews assimilating into the secular Syrian culture in 3rd century B.C. Palestine, and adopting the ways of Gentiles. No one seriously contends that the sect of the Pharisees existed prior to the 3rd century B.C., yet the *Gospel of Barnabas,* Chapter 145, has 17,000 Pharisees existing "in the time of Elijah."

Many more glaring factual and historical errors and absurdities exist in the *Gospel of Barnabas*, and the foregoing samples demonstrate the author's nearly complete lack of understanding of Palestinian geography, New Testament history, and Jewish history. Someone living and writing at the time of Jesus would have never written such absurdities, adding to the proof that the *Gospel of Barnabas* is a 14th century (or, perhaps, 15th century) forgery, and not a very good one at that.

4. Miscellaneous absurdities

Muhammad mentioned by name in a purported 1st century document

Muhammad, the prophet of Islam, is only mentioned four times in the entire Qur'an. So desperate is the Muslim polemicist that forged the *Gospel of Barbabas* that he (or she) included Muhammad's name *fifteen times!* One might ask how the 1st century Barnabas knew that six hundred years later an Arab named Muhammad would emerge and would be considered a prophet. Even more important, if the *Gospel of Barnabas* was actually a 1st century document written by a follower of Jesus, why didn't any Muslim apologists refer to it until well after Toland and Sale identified it in the 17th century?[16] Anyone who accepts that Barnabas in the 1st century wrote about 7th century Muhammad is not exercising faith, but credulity.

5. Conclusions of Islamic scholars

Dr. Shabir Ally

Dr. Ally, one of the best known Islamic scholars in the world, was interviewed about the *Gospel of Barnabas,* and was asked whether it was real or should be "taken with a grain of salt." Dr. Ally responded,

> …I hesitate to use it as an authentic account because the way which Muslims authenticate matters is by having a chain of authority…The chain of authority indicates that the *Gospel of Barnabas* is missing because for many hundreds of years this gospel was not seen anywhere and then suddenly it turned up in the middle ages.[17]

Dr. Muhammad Chafiq Ghurbal

A forged (or Pseudo) Gospel produced by a European in the 15th century; and in its description of the political and religious condition in Palestine at the time of the Messiah, full of errors. For example, it places on the tongue of Isa (Jesus) that he is not the Messiah, but that he came to announce Muhammad who will be the Messiah.[18]

Yusuf Estes

Former Christian preacher and now Muslim preacher Yusuf Estes says regarding the *Gospel of Barnabas,*

> Actually, this is a sad joke on many Muslims. Some have been tricked into believing this has something to do with the New Testament and it is more or less the "Lost Gospel" that will solve all the problems related to the difference between Christianity of today and Islam. But that is all nonsense, because the so-called "Gospel of Barnabas" is "Bogabas" (fake).[19]

Cyril Glasse

> As regards the "Gospel of Barnabas" itself, there is no question that it is a medieval forgery. A complete Italian manuscript exists which appears to be a translation from a Spanish original (which exists in part), written to curry favor with Muslims of the time. It contains anachronisms which can date only from the Middle Ages and not before, and shows a garbled comprehension of Islamic doctrines, calling the Prophet "the Messiah", which Islam does not claim for him. Besides its farcical notion of sacred history, stylistically it is a mediocre parody of the Gospels, as the writings of Baha'Allah are of the Koran.[20]

Conclusion Regarding the *Gospel of Barnabas*

The so-called *Gospel of Barnabas* is heralded today by some Muslim apologists and polemicists as an authentic 1st century account of Jesus. However, no serious scholar of the New Testament, whether Muslim, Christian or non-Christian, finds this writing credible, since all the evidence points to it as a medieval forgery. There was a spurious writing named *Gospel of Barnabas* known in the 6th century as an apocryphal gospel, but no copy of this writing still exists. What is palmed off as being written by the New Testament figure Barnabas was actually concocted sometime after the year 1300, written in Italian, with literally dozens of anachronisms, factual errors, absurdities, misplacements of persons and misplacements of locations.[21] It was written in an obvious attempt to justify teachings of the Qur'an that contradict the authentic Gospels. Those who use the *Gospel of Barnabas* in support of Islam do an injustice to Islam, because using such a dubious source is an indication that some people will accept anything that supports their beliefs, no matter how outlandish (i.e., "confirmation bias"). A wiser path would be to listen to Islamic scholars such as Shabir Ally and Muhammad Chafiq Ghurbal who reject the authenticity of the *Gospel of Barnabas* based on the evidence. If someone wants to know what Jesus actually said and did, the best sources are the accounts of Matthew, Mark, Luke and John.

ENDNOTES

Chapter One

[1]Gerhard Kittel and Gerhard Friedrich, ed., *Theological Dictionary of the New Testament* (Grand Rapids: Eerdmans, 1964), 879.

[2]Shabir Ally, *Is Jesus God? The Bible Says No* (Riyadh, Saudi Arabia: Dar Al-Hadyan, 1997), 10.

Chapter Two

[1]*The American Heritage Dictionary*, 4th ed. (New York: Dell Publishing, 2001), 664.

[2]Matthew 9:2-9; Mark 2:1-12; Luke 5:17-26

[3]Luke 5:24

[4]For those who follow the game of poker, this would be called going "all in."

[5]Luke 5:25

[6]Jehovah's Witnesses are taught that Jesus is Michael the Archangel.

[7]Ibid, 30.

[8]Greek *exousia* "liberty or power to act" G. Abbott-Smith, *A Manual Greek Lexicon of the New Testament*, 3d ed (Edinburgh: T. & T. Clark, 1937), 161.

Chapter Three

[1]The American Heritage Dictionary, 4th ed. New York: Dell Publishing, 2001, 938.

[2]*New American Standard Bible* (Nashville: Thomas Nelson, 1977).

[3]William Arndt and F. Wilbur Gingrich, *A Greek Lexicon of the New Testament and Other Early Christian Literature* (Chicago: University of Chicago Press, 1957), 723-724.

[4]*Proskuneo* is also the Greek word used in Exodus 20:5 ("worship") when the Jews translated the Hebrew Old Testament into Greek (called the "Septuagint") in about the year 250 B.C.

Chapter Four

[1]E.g., Matthew 8:20; 9:6; 10:23, 11:19, 12:8, 12:32, 12:40. 13:37, etc. (78 times in the Gospels).

[2]For an in-depth study of Christ's pre-existence in the Gospels of Matthew, Mark and Luke, see S. J. Gathercole, *The Preexistent Son: Recovering the Christologies of Matthew, Mark, and Luke* (Grand Rapids: Eerdmans, 2006).

Chapter Five

[1]I.e., What Muhammad said, did, approved or disapproved

[2]Exposition of Holy Scripture (Public Domain) accessed 1-2-17 https://www.studylight.org/commentaries/mac/1-corinthians-1.html

Chapter Nine

[1]For the minority view that it is not a hymn, see Gordon D. Fee, *"Philippians 2:5-11: Hymn or Exalted Pauline Prose?"* Bulletin for Biblical Research 2 (1992), 29-46.

Chapter Ten

[1]For an in-depth treatment of the "Granville Sharp Rule," see Daniel B. Wallace, *Greek Grammar Beyond the Basics* (Grand Rapids: Zondervan, 1996), 270-290.

Chapter Twelve

[1]The Da Vinci Code (Doubleday: New York, 2003), 233.

[2]*History of the Church*, 3.36.

[3]Eusebius, ibid, 5.5.

[4]Ibid, 10.

Chapter Thirteen

[1]Greek εγω ειμι ο ων

[2]Nominative singular, masculine, present tense participle from ειμι

[3]*New World Translation of the Holy Scriptures* (Brooklyn: Watchtower Bible and Tract Society, 1950), 312.

[4]Hussaini Yusuf Mabera, *The Bible Says Jesus is Not God*, 2d ed. (Kaduna, Nigeria: Sarumedia Publishers, 2016), 41.

[5]Ibid.

[6]Ibid.

Chapter Fourteen

[1]Relative divine attributes include omniscience, omnipotence They are called "relative" because Jesus could still possess them but did not exercise them apart from authority from the Father. Some attributes, e.g., holiness, are not "exercised," but are facets of who God is, and those cannot be held in abeyance. Thus, some attributes are absolute, such as "self-existence" (called *aseity*).

[2]The Latin term for something in a class by itself is *sui generis*, meaning, "not like anything else."

Chapter Fifteen

[1]Cornelius Tacitus, Roman Historian, writing A.D. 110 c. that Jesus was crucified under Pontius Pilate. *Annals*, Book 15, chapter 34.

[2]John Dominic Crossan, *Jesus: A Revolutionary Biography* (New York: HarperCollins 1995), 145.

[3]See also Matthew 16:21, 17:22-23, 20:28 and Luke 9:22.

[4]There are more than 100 references to Jesus that use the terms "death" "dead" or "died."

[5]E.g., theologian R.C. Sproul says "the divine nature isn't capable of experiencing death," whereas some non-Calvinists resolutely state that the Second Person of the Trinity experienced death, but did not cease to exist.

[6]Retrieved from http://www.allreadable.com/052dKkxx December 24, 2016. Zacharias adds that he obtained the Sheikh's permission to quote him.

Chapter Seventeen

[1]Steve Rudd, http://www.bible.ca/trinity/trinity-oneness-unity-plural-of-majesty-pluralis-majestaticus-royal-we.htm, retrieved December 25, 2016.

[2]The covenant name could not be Jehovah because there is no "J" letter or sound in the Hebrew language, and the "J" sound did not exist in any language until around the 9th century A.D.

[3]Gleason L. Archer, *Encyclopedia of Bible Difficulties* (Grand Rapids: Zondervan, 1982), 359.

[4]Archer, ibid, 359.

[5]Zebi Nasi Hirsch Prinz, *The Great Mystery—How Can Three Be One?* (London, 1863), as cited in Robert Morey, *The Trinity: Evidence and Issues* (Iowa Falls, IA: World Bible Publishers, 1996), 96. Prinz was a lecturer in Hebrew at Oxford University.

[6]Watchtower Bible and Tract Society, *Make Sure of All Things* (Brooklyn: Watchtower Bible and Tract Society, 1953), 282.

[7]Mabera, ibid, 53-55.

Chapter Nineteen

[1]In Arabic "confirming" is a translation of the words *ma bayna yahayhi* that literally means, "between your hands."

Muhammad Asad, *The Message of the Qur'an* (Gibraltar: Dar al-Andalus, 1980), Surah 2:42 footnote 33

[3]From the Hadith (meaning "report" or "narrative"). Hadith are written traditions that are said to contain the words and deeds of Muhammad.

[4]Muhammad considered him *fuqaha* (singular *fiqah*) meaning experts in Islamic jurisprudence ("*fiqh*").

[5]Abdullah Saeed, *The Charge of Distortion of Jewish and Christian Scriptures,* The Muslim World, Vol. 92, (Fall 2002), 429. Saeed is Sultan of Oman Professor of Arab and Islamic Studies, University of Melbourne, Australia.

[6]Ibid, 434.

Appendix Two

[1]Scholars differ on the amount of each Gospel written by the traditional authors, with some doubting that any of the Gospels were written by Matthew, Mark, Luke or John. For further study see my book *In Defense of the Gospels,* publication date estimated to be mid-2017.

[2]Gnosticism was a 2nd century cult that combined elements of Christianity, Judaism and mysticism, and was a threat to the early Christian movement. Most 2nd century Christian apologetics addressed the errors of Gnosticism.

[3]Raymond Brown, "The Gnostic Gospels," *The New York Times Book Review,* 20 Jan. 1980, 3.

[4]*Gospel of Barnabas* Chapter 14.

[5]In Latin *Decretum Gelasianum de libris recipiendis et non recipiendis.* The actual date and author of the *Decretum Gelasianum* are in dispute.

[6]F.C. Cotterell, "The Gospel of Barnabas," *Vox Evangelica* 10 (1977), 45.

[7]Edmund Curll, *An Historical Account of the Life and Writing of the Late Eminently Famous Mr. John Toland* (London: J. Roberts, 1722), 147.

[8]George Sale, *The Koran* (1734).

[9]Cotterell, *Ibid,* 45.

[10]*The Gospel of Barnabas,* Edited and Translated from the Italian ms, in the Imperial Library at Vienna (Oxford: Clarendon Press, 1907).

[11]Surah 3:45, Jesus is called *al-masih* in Arabic, derived from Aramaic *meshiha,* which is derived from the Hebrew *mahsiah* ("anointed"). The Greek equivalent is *Christos,* from whence comes the English word *Christ.*

[12]Jesus confessed, and said the truth: 'I am not the Messiah' (Ragg translation, 1907).

[13]Italian *dei falsi e bugiardi.*

[14]*Enclyclopedia Britannica,* "Year of Jubilee," 11-21-2016, accessed on January 31, 2017 at https://www.britannica.com/topic/Year-of-Jubilee.

[15]Melchior, Caspar and Balthazar, with some variations.

[16]The earliest references to the *Gospel of Barnabas* this author could find from Islamic sources are from the mid-19th century.

[17]Interview on "Let the Quran Speak" accessed on January 31, 2017 at https://www.youtube.com/watch?v=KALwiuy5-5I

[18]Cited by Simaan, Aaod, *The Gospel of Barnabas in the Light of History, Reason and Religion* 3d ed/.(Cairo: Publishing and Distribution House of the Episcopal Church) citing Arabic Encyclopedia, *Al Misra* under the heading "Barnabas" as cited in Campbell, William F., M.D. *The Gospel of Barnabas: Its True Value* (Ralwalpindi: Christian Study Centre, 1989), 35.

[19]Islam Newsroom.com, accessed January 31, 2017 at http://www.islamnewsroom.com/news-we-need/730-gospelofbarnabasfactorfake.

[20]*The Concise Encyclopedia of Islam* (New York: Harper & Row, 1989), 64.

[21]For an extensive treatment of the history and errors showing the *Gospel of Barnabas* to be a medieval forgery, see William F. Campbell, *The Gospel of Barnabas—Its True Value* (Upper Darby, PA: Middle East Resources, 1991).

BIBLIOGRAPHY

Abbott-Smith, G. *A Manual Greek Lexicon of the New Testament*, 3d ed. Edinburgh: T. & T. Clark, 1937.

Ally, Shabir. *Is Jesus God? The Bible Says No*. Riyadh, Saudi Arabia: Dar Al-Hadyan, 1997.

Archer, Gleason L. *Encyclopedia of Bible Difficulties*. Grand Rapids: Zondervan, 1982.

Arndt, WIlliam and F. Wilbur Gingrich, *A Greek Lexicon of the New Testament and Other Early Christian Literature*. Chicago: University of Chicago Press, 1957.

Asad, Muhammad. *The Message of the Qur'an*. Gibraltar: Dar al-Andalus Ltd., 1980.

Brown, Dan. *The Da Vinci Code*. Doubleday: New York, 2003.

Raymond Brown, "The Gnostic Gospels," *The New York Times Book Review*, 20 Jan. 1980.

Campbell, William F. *The Gospel of Barnabas—Its True Value*. Upper Darby, PA: Middle East Resources, 1991.

Cotterell, F.C. "The Gospel of Barnabas," *Vox Evangelica* 10, 1977, 45.

Crossan, John Dominic. *Jesus: A Revolutionary Biography*. New York: HarperCollins, 1995.

Curll, Edmund. *An Historical Account of the Life and Writing of the Late Eminently Famous Mr. John Toland*. London: J. Roberts, 1722.

Enclyclopedia Britannica, "Year of Jubilee," 11-21-2016, accessed on January 31, 2017 at https://www.britannica.com/topic/Year-of-Jubilee.

Fee, Gordon D. *"Philippians 2:5-11: Hymn or Exalted Pauline Prose?"* Bulletin for Biblical Research 2 1992, 29-46.

Gathercole, S.J. *The Preexistent Son: Recovering the Christologies of Matthew, Mark, and Luke.* Grand Rapids: Eerdmans, 2006.

Islam Newsroom.com, accessed January 31, 2017 at http://www.islamnewsroom.com/news-we-need/730-gospelofbarnabasfactorfake.

Kittel, Gerhard and Gerhard Friedrich, ed., *Theological Dictionary of the New Testament.* Grand Rapids: Eerdmans, 1964.

Mabera, Hussaini Yusuf. *The Bible Says Jesus is Not God*, 2d ed. Kaduna, Nigeria: Sarumedia Publishers, 2016.

MacLaren, Alexander. *Exposition of Holy Scripture* (Public Domain) accessed 1-2-17 https://www.studylight.org/commentaries/mac/1-corinthians-1.html

Morey, Robert. *The Trinity: Evidence and Issues.* Iowa Falls, IA: World Bible Publishers, 1996.

New American Standard Bible. Nashville: Thomas Nelson, 1977.

Prinz, Zebi Nasi Hirsch. *The Great Mystery—How Can Three Be One?* London, 1863.

Rudd, Steve http://www.bible.ca/trinity/trinity-oneness-unity-plural-of-majesty-pluralis-majestaticus-royal-we.htm, retrieved December 25, 2016.

Sale, George. *The* Koran, 1734.

Simaan, Aaod, *The Gospel of Barnabas in the Light of History, Reason and Religion* 3d ed. Cairo: Publishing and Distribution House of the Episcopal Church, n. d.

The American Heritage Dictionary, 4th ed. New York: Dell Publishing, 2001.

The Concise Encyclopedia of Islam. New York: Harper & Row, 1989.

The Gospel of Barnabas, Edited and Translated from the Italian manuscripts, in the Imperial Library at Vienna. Oxford: Clarendon Press, 1907.

Wallace, Daniel B. Greek Grammar Beyond the Basics. Grand Rapids: Zondervan, 1996.

Watchtower Bible and Tract Society, *Make Sure of All Things.* Brooklyn: Watchtower Bible and Tract Society, 1953.

_____. *New World Translation of the Holy Scriptures.* Brooklyn: Watchtower Bible and Tract Society, 1950.

ABOUT THE AUTHOR

John Stewart is the Executive Director of Ratio Christi International and is a lawyer, Christian apologist, author and award-winning radio personality, holding earned degrees in Biblical Studies, Theological Studies, and Law. John formerly co-hosted the nationally-syndicated radio program "The Bible Answerman" with the late Walter Martin and hosted his own nationally-syndicated radio show, "John Stewart Live." John served as Professor of Law and Apologetics at the Simon Greenleaf School of Law (now Trinity Law School) in California, where he was also Assistant Dean of the Law Program and later served as Assistant Director of the Christian Research Institute in California. He is the author of five books, and has received many awards and recognitions, including an Angel Award for excellence in broadcasting, and was named "Pro-Life Broadcaster of the Year." John testified by invitation as a Protestant Theologian before President George H. W. Bush's Presidential Commission on the Assignment of Women in the Military. He has appeared on local and national television and radio in America and around the world, including CNN, national news on CBS, NBC and ABC, MacNeil-Lehrer and Good Morning America. John has spoken at many colleges, universities and law schools in many countries, and has engaged in numerous debates on college campuses. He has spoken at apologetic ("Intelligent Faith") conferences throughout America, Africa and Asia, and is a visiting scholar at Multnomah Biblical Seminary in Portland, Oregon. John has been a lecturer at Calvary Chapel Bible School Jerusalem, Manna Bible Institute in Nairobi, Kenya, and Hindustan Bible Institute in Chennai, India. John and his wife Laurie are allied attorneys with the Alliance Defending Freedom. For speaking events, contact John through the Ratio Christi website (notifications@ratiochristi.org).